EMBRACING YOUR TRUTH

Asking the Questions That Set You FREE

JOANNA ASHLEY

Copyright ©2014 by JoAnna Ashley
Cover and Internal design © by Dream Team Publishers
Cover Design by JP Creative

All rights reserved. No part of this book may be reproduced in any form or by any electronic or mechanical means including information storage and retrieval systems – except in the case of brief quotations embodied in critical articles or reviews – without the permission in writing from its publisher, Dream Team Publishers.

This publication is designed to provide accurate and authoritative information in regard to the subject matter. It is sold with the understanding that the publisher or author is not engaged in rendering legal, accounting, or other professional service. If legal advice or other expert assistance is required, the services of a competent, professional person should be sought. – *From a Declaration of Principles Jointly Adopted by a Committee of the American Bar Association and a Committee of Publishers and Associations*

This book is not intended as a substitute for medical advice from a qualified physician. The intent of this book is to provide accurate general information in regard to the subject matter covered. If medical advice or other expert help is needed, the services of an appropriate medical professional should be sought.

All brand names and product names used in this book are trademarks, registered trademarks, or trade names of their respective holders. Dream team Publishers is not associated with any product or vendor in this book.

This book contains content and stories from the author which represents the author's present recollection of her experiences over a period of years. Some names and characters have been changed, some events have been compressed and some dialogue has been re-created.

Published by Dream Team Publishers
P.O. Box 734, Vacaville CA, 95696
(707) 514-0418
www.dreamteampublishers.com

ISBN 978-0-9885609-2-5

Library of Congress Cataloguing-in-Publication data is on file with the Publisher

Printed and bound in the United States of America
10   9   8   7   6   5   4   3   2   1

This book is dedicated to those who give us the love, freedom, support and trust to help us soar in life. Adam, my love, you have given all this and more. Thanks for letting me soar. I love you.

Acknowledgments

This is where I am supposed to acknowledge those who have helped me along the way. However, I want *you* take this moment instead and think of all those who have helped you along your way. Our gratitude and love to those who have helped us most is the greatest gift we can give. Acknowledge those in your life who have played a part in helping you succeed.

Now for me to acknowledge those who have helped me. First, my husband, Adam, and children, Bobbie Jo and Gabriel. Your love, patience, encouragement and support have carried me through the moments when I wanted to give up most. I live each day in the vision of creating the life of our dreams as we help others create the life of their dreams.

To my family, both blood and spiritually adopted, who have helped me, loved me and supported me along the way, thank you. Katrina and Moria, your total love and support of me as well as your willingness to love and care for my children when I have had to work and travel means more to me than you will ever know, thank you. Rosa, your faith in me and my gifts has helped me time and time again. Mom and Dad, thank you for believing in me, helping me along the way and loving me always despite not always understanding my path.

Melanie, Miko and Lisa, thank you for being my grounding crew. You have each been so vital in helping me discover who I am and what I have to offer the world. Your countless hours of love, counsel, unconditional support and willingness to open my eyes to even the not-so-great aspects of myself have been immeasurable for helping me soar.

Lydia and Bobbie K., thank you for being my examples of going after what it is I want most and not settling for no. You have helped me embrace my inner backbone, take a stance in my life, declare what it is I want and then go after it. Verena, thank you for being one of the first to love me and support me as I began to find myself.

To my Creator and Universe, thank you for so gloriously orchestrating all the events and introductions that have occurred and made this all possible. I love each of you and all of you not mentioned who have played many vital roles in my life, from the bottom of my heart, thank you and I am forever grateful for all you have done for me. Love, Jo.

Foreword

Bob and I are leaders in the transformation industry in our own right. Bob was featured in the movie *The Secret* and has offered transformational programs since the year 2000. I've been in the entertainment business as a TV and Radio Host and transitioned into the personal growth field in 2002. Together, he and I personally know and have worked with almost every well-known leader in that world—and have personally experienced healing and transformational work from around the globe.

In addition, for the last two years, we've turned our expertise and success toward helping launch mission-driven entrepreneurs and experts to leading status in their industries. We've been blessed to work with many heart-centered souls and the beautiful work and service they bring to the planet. We feel lucky to be part of their journey and even luckier to experience their work.

A couple of years ago, we had the honor of meeting and working with JoAnna, and she rocked our world. Her pure heart, her amazing story and the simplicity of her process combined with the power of its instant effectiveness and lasting change were stunning to witness.

As you read this book, you too will be in awe of what she's been through and how she turned herself around as well as what she discovered in the process that has now been helping so many lives (including ours).

We initially met JoAnna at a program we spoke at in October, 2012, where she signed up to work with us. Through the process of helping her write and produce training videos for her program, along with helping to chart out her brand, we were moved by the sincere love she has for others. She possessed the desire to help everyone she met grow and heal beyond the hurts, heartaches, and struggles in their lives, and we knew she was someone special and someone to watch.

We were floored to learn that at such a young age she overcame so much only to immediately turn around and help others do the same. When we met JoAnna, she was only twenty-five and she'd already overcome fibromyalgia, arthritis, infertility, suicidal depression, diabetes, and so many other ailments. It was astounding to comprehend how she suffered through so much at such a young age.

As we learned more and worked with her, we got to see firsthand her passion to free people from the torments of their pasts that kept them sick, broken, and stuck. During that time, she even offered profound advice for both of us in the physical and emotional issues we were facing. Thanks to her process and her calm nature, an instant shift occurred as she tuned in, got right to the core, and gently released the blocks.

We know in this book JoAnna has done her best to bring you true hope and knowledge about how to heal and change your life. Plus she's sprinkled it with her famous analogies and perspectives to make your journey fun and easy.

JoAnna, in her sincerity and transparency, is refreshing and inspiring. She's unafraid of her past and her future. As result, she has a vivacious zest for life and healing. In her humble yet courageous way, she inspires others to embrace their lives with love, knowledge, courage and empowerment to create their very best lives. With her contagious attitude and spirit, she has done a stellar job connecting you to experience the most extraordinary healing transformation of your life.

After finishing this book, you will be more grounded, more alive, more passionate, more peaceful and balanced, and best of all, happy and healthy.

Enjoy and get ready for a heart-centered, healing adventure!

Lynn and Bob

Table of Contents

Introduction..1

Chapter 1: Fear and Hurt or Love and
Faith Are the Only Ways We Can Exist.......................6
   Love Is Expanding Energy
   Fear Is a Contracting Force
   Empowerment Happened When I Chose My Truth
   Tool One: All You Need Is Love
   Hannah's Story

Chapter 2: Healing Begins within You.........................18
   Spiritual Body
   Emotional Body
   Mental Body
   Physical Body
   The Four Bodies in Balance

Chapter 3: What's True For You, Is True for You........31
   Authentically Living Your Truth
   Living in the Moment
   Not Everything Is Black and White
   Living Life with Your Beliefs
   Discovering Your Truth
   Tool Two: Exploring What's True for You

Chapter 4: Your Emotions and Beliefs
Create the Rules You Live By.......................................44
   Good Feelings and Thoughts Create a Good Reality
   Tool Three: Create Your Reality through Your Emotions and Beliefs
   Karen's Story

Chapter 5: Your Body Is a Map..51
    Discovering the Root Cause Will Heal the Body and Soul
    Emotions of the Skeletal Structure
    Emotions of the Organs
    Healing Our Bodies Is a Cooperative Effort
    Tool Four: Mapping Your Body

Chapter 6: Nothing is Impossible for You........................70
    Your Creative Imagination Is the Key to Life
    Your Emotional Response Creates Your Outcome
    Tool Five: Do the Impossible
    Eliza's Story

Chapter 7: Your Feelings and Thoughts Create Your Life. Use Them..84
    You Give Your Feelings and Thoughts Power
    Your Feelings and Thoughts Are the Key to Life
    Tool Six: Use Your Feelings and Thoughts to Create
    Lane's Story

Chapter 8: The Key to Change Is Shifting from Judgment to Compassion..95
    Love Repairs the Unrepairable
    Compassion Is for You, Too
    Tool Seven: A Life of Compassion

Chapter 9: The Answers to all Your Questions Exist Within...........109
    Change Your Beliefs and Change Your Emotional Response
    Fear Is a Dream Snatcher
    The Universe Is Waiting for You
    Love Energy Flows through You
    Give Yourself Permission to Be Truthful
    The Truth within Will Guide You
    Your Faith Heals You
    You Have the Power to Do Something about It
    Tool Eight: Finding the Answers within You
    Your Higher Purpose Is in the Expression of You
    Empower Yourself and Live Your Truth

Introduction

Whatever the reason you picked up this book, I want you, dear reader, to know I wrote these words for you. I poured my heart and soul into these pages in hopes that by the finale you'll truly be able to embrace your life's truth, healing and growing in ways you never even thought possible!

The greatest tragedy of our day is so many of us live on autopilot. We do the very best we can just to get through one day, climb into bed, and hope we can survive tomorrow. We bounce through the struggles, crawl through the sicknesses, and work ourselves ragged to make ends meet. We desperately hope someday, maybe, things *might* actually get better.

I want to assure you, my friend, your circumstances can certainly improve, and it doesn't require vast sums of money to do so. If you put your fears, doubts, and insecurities on a shelf for a few moments and genuinely put forth an effort to apply what I share with you, it won't be long before you see wonderful changes in your life.

My hope is you'll embrace this book as a guide to finally make extraordinary changes in your life. The best part? The only requirements are some concentrated effort and a little touch of hope and faith.

You can look forward to learning how to let the past go and move forward in your life from a place of strength and confidence. You'll find a place of safety within yourself where you can begin looking at the beliefs you've adopted and whether or not they're true for you. You'll see how every event stems from only two forces, love or fear, and how both forces radically affect your life. I'll show you how your emotions and feelings (not just your thoughts) create your life. Together, we'll begin unlocking the chains that keep you trapped and limited. As you open the door of unlimited opportunities for your life, you'll find nothing is impossible. Compassion for yourself and others will become your foundational key to healing wounds and bringing genuine wholeness into your life. You'll discover your body truly is a blessing, and you'll learn how to understand the language of disease, hurt and aches your body speaks. This understanding will open the doorway to unlimited physical healing. Finally you'll see how to find all the answers to your questions within you.

My friend, this book will move you spiritually, energetically, and emotionally to places you may have never been before. I encourage you to stay the course regardless of how new, scary, or uncomfortable it may feel.

Life begins at the end of your comfort zone.
–Neale Donald Walsch

The life you seek, the healing you crave, and the happiness and success that beckons in your dreams are waiting just on the other side of your comfort zone. This book will push you to the very edge of your comfort zone and beyond, right onto the doorstep of the life you seek. Whether or not you choose to take the steps up to the front door and enter into the life you've desperately sought will be determined by the actions you take after reading this book.

At the end of each chapter, I've provided extremely powerful, life-altering tools. They may seem simplistic; however, don't let their simplicity deceive you. They have the power to completely alter your life and world. Additionally, I've created an expanded, more in-depth version of each tool, giving you your own mini coaching sessions with me. You can access this expanded material free online at

http://www.joannaashley.com/embracing-your-truth/

The material in this book can change your life, just as it transformed mine. My desire is that you read, learn, and apply these powerful concepts and then share this book with someone special in your life who's also seeking positive change.

I crave to be an example and teach others how to live light and free—free from emotional baggage, from false beliefs and perceptions that hold us captive. My desire is to firmly plant self-love, compassion, hope, and inspiration into the life of every single, beautiful soul I meet. I love you and want you to know the world needs *you* in your place of truth, wholeness, health, and love. Courageously share your greatness, unfiltered and unhampered, from anything in your past or current circumstances. The world needs *you fully living in your truth!*

Get ready to embark upon an amazing journey of freedom. I hope you'll share your stories of transformation and healing with me. I look forward to hearing from you.

I wrote this book for you from a place of experience. Every chapter was woven from the threads that have created the tapestry of my life. I've personally gone through, struggled with, and overcome everything I'll teach you here. Not only have I transformed my life by what I'll teach you, but I've helped countless others transform theirs as well; some of whose stories you'll get to read.

To begin this book, before diving into the principles I teach, I want to give you an anchor point and experience to help you understand the possibilities this book has in store for you and your life.

I'm going to describe a woman to you, and based on my description, I want you to do the best you can to guess her age. This woman has become extremely limited in her physical abilities. Arthritis has grabbed hold of her hands so strongly she cannot open anything with a lid or lace her shoes without the help of her husband. At one time in her life, she could play the piano for hours, but now she's lucky if her body can withstand sitting to play a single song.

Her body is so sensitive she can feel oncoming storms deep within her joints and muscles four to six days before they even arrive. Every morning she wakes, having to do a body check. What body parts will work today and which are the most painful? At this time camping, hiking, and outdoor activities look like hobbies of her past. She loves the people who matter in her life, but most days she cannot stand being touched or hugged. She has so many allergies her diet is greatly restricted, and she has only a few options of safe food. Her memory is poor—she forgets people's names, what she did the day before, and she walks into a room four to five times hoping she'll remember why she's there. She's afraid of being alone and often asks herself, "What could possibly be my purpose in life?" Because of her physical condition, it's nearly impossible for her to have children.

How old do you think this woman is? Perhaps sixty years old? Maybe seventy? How about seventy-five years old? Actually, this was me at age twenty. I was married just over a year and half to my love, Adam, and my life was quickly unravelling around me. These were only some of my symptoms of living with an array of illnesses that included fibromyalgia, arthritis, allergies, crippling anxiety, panic attacks, and infertility. However, all this began to change the day I visited a woman who candidly asked me, "Do you want it?"

I was floored by her question. Of course I didn't want it, but what choice did I have? After all, I was told and believed fibromyalgia was incurable, arthritis could only be managed, and my memory would probably get worse over time. It was a daily game of trying to retain my memory and workable body parts. My response to her question was, "No! But I don't have a choice, do I?"

Her response, "I don't care. Do you want the fibromyalgia?"

Again, I replied, "No."

She smiled and said, "Then I can help you."

This was the beginning of my journey to healing and my journey to self-discovery and the unveiling of my truth. Little did I know then that today I'd be cured of fibromyalgia, arthritis, diabetes, memory loss, allergies, anxiety, fear, and infertility. I'm transformed and have realized I'm master of my fate and captain of my soul. I create and heal my life. Although my story is unique, it's not unusual because we all have the divinely given right to create, heal, and live the life we choose. You too have this innate ability to tap into the gift that's already yours.

You're unique unto yourself, and accepting another's truth as your own without investigating first can cause frustration and upset. To rise above the crowd, look within and garner the courage to consult yourself on anything in the doorway to freedom, happiness, and wholeness. You're more right than you realize. Give yourself credit. In the pages of this book you'll discover how I made the gentle but powerful changes that transformed my health and my life and how you can do it, too.

1
Fear and Hurt or Love and Faith Are the Only Ways We Can Exist

"*Every action taken by human beings is based in love or fear, not simply those dealing with relationships. Decisions affecting business, industry, politics, religion, the education of your young, the social agenda of your nations, the economic goals of your society, choices involving war, peace, attack, defense, aggression, submission; determinations to covet or give away, to save or to share, to unite or to divide-every single free choice you ever undertake arises out of one of the only two possible thoughts there are: a thought of love or a thought of fear.*

Fear is the energy which contracts, closes down, draws in, runs, hides, hoards, harms.

Love is the energy which expands, opens up, sends out, stays, reveals, shares, and heals.

Fear wraps our bodies in clothing; love allows us to stand naked. Fear clings to and clutches all that we have; love gives all that we have away. Fear holds close, love holds dear. Fear grasps, love lets go. Fear rankles, love soothes. Fear attacks, love amends.

Every human thought, word, or deed is based in one emotion or the other. You have no choice about this, because there is nothing else from which to choose. But you have free choice about which of these to select."

–Neale Donald Walsch from *Conversations with God*

This excerpt simplifies life a great deal, doesn't it? One of the greatest struggles in many of our lives is overcomplicating things, making it feel impossible to change anything. However, when you realize everything in life stems from love or fear, it quickly becomes easy to realize which one is the motivating force in your life. For many, it seems nearly impossible to overcome fear because it has such a strong, powerful presence in their lives. The overwhelming sense of anxiety within you feels real. It may be felt through a racing heart, sweaty palms, and an overload of thoughts. How can you possibly harness and eliminate your fear when it seems almost larger than you? Living a fear-driven life is futile to your success. Fear serves a purpose—when there's an immediate threat or danger in our environment, like a thief or a presence that can endanger your well-being. The fight or flight response is engaged in the body allowing you to respond accordingly and protect yourself. However, when fear is the primary, most powerful motivator to making decisions, it can only make your life miserable over and over every time it dominates your thoughts and feelings.

  Fear is a restriction of Love Energy and can leave you emotionally paralyzed. Consider this, when you fear something, you stop in your tracks, freeze, and allow it to consume you. Or, you may run away from it and never confront the root of your problem. Feelings and thoughts are the energetic forces influencing your mental and physical health more than any other single factor. The quality of your feelings and thoughts determine your physical and emotional condition. If you're thinking and feeling positively and you're optimistic and determined, you'll naturally attract good things into your life because you're opening the pathways to allow Love Energy to flow abundantly through you, bringing growth and healing. When your feelings and thoughts are fear-based, such as anger or doubt, you'll manifest situations that resonate with anger or doubt because the flow of Love Energy has been restricted creating destruction and chaos. Energy vibrates and attracts like energy. So if you're using love, hope and compassion to create and experience your life, you'll get exactly this. It's the same way for fear. You'll simply attract more fear into your life and your experiences.

In her book, *You Can Heal Your Life*, Louise Hay eloquently states, *Every thought we think is creating our future. Each one of us creates our experiences by our thoughts and our feelings. The thoughts we think and the words we speak create our experiences.*

Your future is in your hands. It's always been true. The ability to create what you want from life is in your feelings, thoughts, and the words you speak. You can choose love or fear; it's your decision, and as with any decision, there's a consequence. You determine this, too.

My whole life I struggled with deep-seated, fear-based emotions. I truly was almost afraid of my own shadow. There were many reality-based fears such as money and even relationships. Then I had many completely irrational fears stemming from the abuse and other experiences I had in my life. Until I was roughly twenty-one, my life was paralyzed by fear. My actions and the course of my life were determined by how much fear I felt. If anything became uncomfortable, I ran. As a result, I ran away from a lot of fantastic opportunities because I interpreted my fear as my Creator saying, "No." Once I started taking control of my fear by embracing the Love Energy from my Creator, doorways started opening for me, and I started experiencing a great deal of success.

Love is Expanding Energy

What's love, really? We use the word "love" a great deal to express our feelings toward another person or even an object. Such as, "I love that house," or, "I love those shoes." This is what I call "Love the concept." I don't mean to diminish what you feel when you say you love a person or when you say you love something. However, the use of the word "love" in these scenarios is a description of an emotion you feel towards someone or something. It doesn't truly carry much power in the energy perspective of things.

However when you recognize love is actually a moving, creating force in the Universe, you then begin to realize the power of creation and healing we all have in our lives. I refer to this kind of love as *Love Energy*, which you'll recognize. I've used this term previously. When someone says, "I'm sending love your way," this isn't just a nice thought or lovely words to say they care. It's actually the person sending a powerful, positive, and compassionate energy force towards you to create a positive change. Love Energy is always expanding and growing bigger and greater. Energy is all around us, and the source of that energy is love which is everywhere and in everything. Love heals, unifies, and covers all wrongdoings or hurts. Love is the reason why birds sing, lovers kiss, and babies smile. Just look and see—you'll find love everywhere around you. It's the creative force in the Universe; all life is created from this Love Energy.

One of the great ways to grow and expand your Love Energy is by removing the need to control the "hows" in your life. Decide what it is you desire and begin by asking yourself what it would be like to experience that very thing. I've found that asking questions is one of the most valuable tools given to us. This is why the tools toward the end of almost all the chapters are provocative questions that will hopefully make you think in a slightly different way in order to spark the healing of your mind, body, emotions, or spirit. This is because the questions are about getting your Mental Body out of the way so your Spiritual Body can unleash its unlimited Love Energy on your Emotional Body to create healing. When you see that healing manifest in your Physical Body or physical world, it's an incredible thing indeed.

In the book *The Magic in Asking the Right Questions* by Bill Mayer, the author gives a series of fantastic little questions that can help you see your world and your circumstances in a different way immediately helping you grow love, success, and expansiveness. Mayer writes:

> *Consistently ask yourself empowering questions and you'll be amazed at how quickly you'll develop positive habits that guarantee a good, if not great, day every day. Situations will dictate the right questions to ask yourself.*

There are twenty empowering questions I ask myself on a regular basis. Without a doubt, they put magic in my life. Be aware the empowering questions you create and use don't have to always be lengthy or profound–simplicity is often effective. Discover the magic in asking the right questions as you apply some of these questions in your life. My twenty favorite questions are:

1. How can I **make it fun**?
2. What's **great** about this?
3. What am I **thankful** for?
4. What's **a better way** of looking at this?
5. What's my **desired outcome**?
6. What's a **possible solution**?
7. What did I **learn** from this?
8. How can I **simplify** this?
9. What would a **Power Thinker** do in this situation?
10. What's the **best use of my time** right now?
11. What **actions** do I need to take?
12. **Why** do I want to do this?
13. What are the **benefits**?
14. How can I **feel better** right now?
15. How can I **raise my energy** level?
16. What do I want to **accomplish today**?
17. How can I be more **productive**?
18. What do I **value** most in my life?
19. What's a **better choice** to focus on?
20. What's a **more empowering question** to ask?

These questions are a fantastic starting point to begin proactively seeing your world differently, which in turn will open countless doorways to new possibilities and solutions.

Fear Is a Contracting Force

The nemesis or opposite of Love Energy is fear which is the absence of love. Fear is always a contracting force, growing smaller and tighter, the opposite of expansion. Fear encompasses everything negative within us. Doubt, resentment, anger, blame, frustration, sadness—it's all there. Fear traps us in outdated thought patterns that don't work and no longer bear fruit. When we use fear or negativity, we agree to use emotional mental loops that pull us down and drain our energy. This negativity and limiting beliefs stop the flow of Love Energy. As a result it stops us from feeling peace, prosperity, mental fortitude, etc. What we focus on, we give power to.

If we choose our limiting beliefs based on fear, it's time-consuming and uses our imagination in negative ways to create the worst possible outcome because it restricts the flow of creation from the Love Energy. A mask fear often wears is anxiety which creates the worst possible thoughts about something that may or may not happen in the future. Whether fear is imagined or real, our body still may respond to it by sweating, increasing our heart rate, and tensing our muscles. Ultimately, fear kicks you out of present time, meaning you become less aware of your current environment because you're consumed by some ill-fated, future event that may never happen.

Bruce Doyle III, Ph.D. is a formerly successful executive with General Electric. After leaving his corporate career at GE, he chose to dedicate himself and his work to helping people step away from their limiting beliefs like fear and step toward a reality that helps them achieve the purposeful success they always imagined but never believed was truly possible. In his book, *How to Think Your Way to the Life You Want*, Doyle writes:

> *What do you think is really believed by a man who affirms fifty times a day, 'I'm rich! I'm rich! I'm rich!' You guessed it; he really believes that he is not rich.*
>
> *He is also strengthening the thought form that is already keeping him from being rich. He'll soon see no results for his efforts and give up in frustration. His limiting belief could have to do with*

money, but most often it's a personal belief, such as the belief that he does not deserve money or a related belief.

One of the lessons I had to learn the hard way when I began exploring belief systems was that experiences are determined by the sum total of your beliefs and your point of mental focus, your attention—not just the experiences you selectively choose to create. I decided that since I had all this profound knowledge of how the Universe works, I would get up the next morning and simply create what I wanted. Well, it didn't work, and as you might guess, I generated a lot of frustration and anger for myself. I guess I had a transparent belief about how I learn things—the hard way.

As we've seen, beliefs can be empowering or limiting. Limiting beliefs negate or subtract from empowering beliefs and desires. What do you get when you add +2 and -2? You're right—zero!

Fear is mankind's worse enemy ever. Left unattended, fear can suffocate your finances, your passion, and your purpose because it literally squeezes the life force of Love Energy out of you.

On the flip side, with love you can reach new heights of fulfillment, joy, satisfaction, and peace. Fear is a part of the human experience for most people, but when left unattended it will strangle you and choke off the oxygen of fresh ideas and positive thoughts. Although I still occasionally fear some things, I'm able to control how and what I focus my time and energy on. As a result I quickly open my being back up to the flow of Love Energy.

Before I understood the polar opposite dynamics of love and fear, to a large degree I believed chaos ruled the Universe. *Things just happened for no apparent rhyme or reason,* I thought. I believed unpredictability and randomness was simply a way of life. I always operated from the reactive mind rather than with a conscious, responding mindset. Yes, things do happen beyond our realm of control at times, it's true. However, living in a reactive state attracts negativity; it's typical of living in a world that restricts the flow of Love Energy. Believing chaos is always Lord Almighty, we're unable to accept responsibility for our own destiny. In fact it's impossible. People who hold this belief system haplessly give their thoughts over to emotional baggage that cannot do anything for them except drag them down.

Empowerment Happened When I Chose My Truth

When we're hurting and haven't yet healed our own lives, we're not emotionally available to truly help anyone else in a substantive way. When I began trusting my inner truth and consulting with my Creator and the Universe through the use of the questions, I started unleashing a drastic and rapid life transformation. I was able to shift my focus much more quickly and open my being, allowing an abundance of Love Energy to flow through me bringing new solutions, new perspectives, and healing.

Back in the 300s AD, decisions were made by the newly forming Christian church authorities about which gospels written by the disciples were to be included in the Bible and which were to be left out for eternity. Those scriptures left out were given to monks in the desert who were instructed to burn them. Instead, the monks sealed twelve leather bound volumes in several jars and they were buried not far from their monastery. In 1945, a local farmer discovered the jars and the contents within that were supposed to have been burned almost two millennia ago.

The gospel, or writings, according to Thomas, also known as "doubting Thomas" were decreed as "heretical" and left out of the Bible because they questioned the notion of faith and Christianity as looking outward to find God.

Instead, these writings surprisingly suggested we look within for answers to the challenges we face rather than always looking outward to a god that exists up in the heavens somewhere. In the interest of full disclosure—some people consider the Gnostic Gospels as fakes. I will leave those discussions to historians. But even the possibility that words were written back in those ancient days with the notion of empowering people and encouraging them to seek their own solutions is exciting.

Understanding they were purposefully left out of the scriptures we know today is revealing. Ancient authorities who formed the church seemed to want people to remain dependent on outside forces rather than develop a belief and faith in themselves, seeking their own truth and trusting themselves to find the answers they seek.

I was realizing our primary choice in life is love or fear. From this, we manifest the reality of the emotions by which we choose to live. Naturally, we're full of energy to create what we give power to day by day. So if you're living in a place of fear, your focus will create more fear. If you're living in a place of love, your focus will create more love and expansion. You have the ability to create your truth with the highest power which is love, and it comes directly from our Creator and the Universe. You can face the events in your life with truth and confidence by simply asking, "How can I look at this with love?" For example, putting this book together is a manifestation of love. Instead of going into a state of fear and doubt, "I cannot do this," I started visualizing in my mind and spirit what it would be like to do it and bring it to fruition.

At one time I felt isolated and cut off from God. I felt He didn't hear my prayers. I believed I was unworthy and was destined to live a life of suffering and pain. The hidden truth of the Universe is it responds to our thoughts. If we advocate joy, peace, wealth, and healing, the Universe opens the door to opportunity for positive experiences. The same is true of fear. If we support worry and entertain anxiety, the Universe responds to our emotional tone and delivers exactly what we focus our energy upon. At one time I was living in a way others told me would cut me off from God. I believed them, and the emotions and beliefs in my Emotional Body orchestrated events that confirmed it must be exactly what was happening. I was so sick, my finances were falling apart. I got the exact opposite of what I prayed for. Surely with such horrible happenings I had lost the favor of God, or so I thought.

However knowing what I know now, none of it was happening because I was truly cut off from God. Rather it was happening because I *believed* I'd been cut off from God, thus cutting off the flow of Love Energy that would create beautiful, wonderful things and happenings in my life. Our beliefs are incredibly powerful and potent things, creating in every moment we focus upon.

Within you are the answers. Within you is the *why* you're here, *how* to get what you need for your purpose, and how to heal any aberration or irregularity stealing you away from your calling. Your life can be the ideal testimony to inspire others on their journey. As I've shared with you, my life is a testament to the power of reaching out to experts who guided me on the path to heal myself and create a meaningful life filled with peace, hope, and satisfaction.

Through my experiences working with clients and studies of an array of several different Energy Healing modalities and processes, I couldn't find what my soul was seeking. As a result, and purely by accident, I realized I'd developed a powerful, unique program creating results unlike I'd seen before in such a short amount of time. I came to call this process Mach IV Transformation Series which utilizes the amazingly simple but powerful tool I created called GABE. It means Ground, Align, Balance and Excel. GABE is a healing method or system that can transform your life instantaneously. It's the foundation for all the tools I provide you in this book. Not only do I use this method to get instant results for any issues or antagonism in my own life, but I've shared it many times with my healing clients to help them find relief and greater stability for their journey. I'm sharing this tool with you now because *your* transformation and healing is my utmost goal.

Below you'll find Tool One to help you experience the power of this transformative healing system crafted to your specific needs, wants, and desires. The structure of this tool is the same structure you'll see throughout all the tools I provide you in this book.

Tool One: All You Need Is Love

- First, imagine a peaceful place. I call this your brain vacation spot.
- Next, out loud ask the question: "What does it feel like to come to a neutral place regarding this situation?" Immediately afterward put your brain on vacation. Don't try thinking of an answer to the question; just enjoy your brain vacation.
- Once you're done shifting to a place of neutrality ask yourself, "What do I want to happen? How do I want this situation resolved?"
- When you ask these questions, immediately write down what comes to mind, even if it's one or two sporadic words. Or if an image comes to mind, describe it. Write down the result you desire in great detail.
- Finally, after you've pictured exactly what you want and you can *feel* what that outcome will feel like, ask yourself, "What does it feel like to shift and align all my emotions and belief system to be in harmony with the outcome I want?"

I have a mini coaching session tool and additional tools available at my website. You can access them at:

http://www.joannaashley.com/embracing-your-truth/

Go to Chapter 1 resources.

Hannah's story.

I met Hannah who had a great deal of negative experiences in her young life. From the time she was a young girl, she believed fear was the only way to live. She believed it was natural to walk around feeling scared, worrying over everything that happened to her and fearing everything that could possibly happen. Hannah's life was a video of fear-filled experiences. Finances would get tight and she would get scared trying to figure out how to fix them. The more scared she became, the more destitute her financial situation became.

I soothingly started introducing Hannah to the notion that, by changing her focus from fear to love, she could change her life for the better. We had to take it slowly because one of the traits that kept Hannah alive and going for so long was a willingness and need to fight change. Often she discovered she was fighting against the exact same thing she wanted and didn't even realize it.

As time progressed and we continued working together, opportunities started presenting themselves to Hannah to see if she would or could shift her focus from fear to love. She would make a mistake in her financial budgeting and suddenly she would come up short on money. I'd gently step in and give her a few questions to ask herself so she could see it differently and reinforce the positive change she said she wanted. The moment Hannah shifted her focus away from fear to one of love, that was the moment her situation would begin turning around and money would start seeping out of the woodwork for her.

These days Hannah is a powerful, persuasive advocate for the notion that your focus will change the outcome of your life whether the question is about finances, relationships, or dealing with children. She no longer allows the bumps in the road of life get her off track because she realizes now the faster she turns to love, the faster she begins building her dreams again.

2
Healing Begins within You

You, like so many others, are on a quest for answers and solutions in your life. Like others, you've searched many avenues to find them. Maybe you've looked at self-help programs in your religion and spiritual texts. You have even paid someone a great deal of money to help you find answers and healing in your life. You may have experienced some answers and even some healing, but you're still left with more unanswered questions and a craving to understand life. I know, I've been there and it can be extremely frustrating and discouraging. However, I've got fantastic news. You're about to find your answers.

Now that you understand the two forces of all life, love and fear, you have a simple foundation upon which to build your life. The simplicity of this knowledge alone brings so many solutions because it's easy to see what direction you're going. When in doubt or facing confusion, take a moment and ask yourself, "Does this situation/decision/moment make me feel love or fear?" If it brings fear, you know you must do something different, and if you feel love, you know you're on the right track.

The next foundational piece for finding answers as well as healing and transforming your life begins by understanding *who* you are. What creates the very being of you? I've found each of us beautiful human beings are actually made up of four parts, or as I see it, each of our *beings* are made up out of the combination of *four bodies* within us—Spiritual, Emotional, Mental and Physical Body. In our lives, each of these bodies are responsible for various functions so we can create and live our lives filled with love, peace, fulfillment, joy, and so much more. As you begin understanding the role that each of these bodies play in your life, you'll begin to better understand what is creating the problems. As a result, you'll begin finding solutions for your life!

The Spiritual Body

The Spiritual Body is your spirit, but also it's your spiritual and energetic connection to everyone and everything. This is the place where you're connected to every other living being in the Universe as well as to God, Creator, the Universe, Mother Earth— whatever you believe. This is the body in which you're directly connected with the Love Energy source that creates all life, abundance, and wholeness. This is the facet of you that all things in your life come from. You can look at the Spiritual Body as *the genie for your life*; your wish is its command. Now I know you may be skeptical of this, especially if your life has been filled with lots of struggle, heartache, and illnesses, but I assure you it's true. You'll be able to understand more as I expand your understanding on the other three bodies here in just a moment.

Your Spiritual Body is where all things are created. This Spiritual Body is where your intuition comes from, where the ability to just know things without having researched them, where all knowledge, insight, and direction for your life comes from. If you're looking for answers, seeking peace or comfort, or looking for love, this is the place where all these things and so much more are created and then delivered to you. You can essentially think of your Spiritual Body as your crystal ball carrying, unconditionally loving, all caring, inspiration giving, best friend who believes in you no matter what and wants the best for you in everything!

Indicators that your Spiritual Body is your dominant body:

When the Spiritual Body is out of balance and playing the dominant, ruling role in your life, you may be rather detached from reality. You float through life trying to not be too attached to the outcomes, so more often than not you don't make plans and just settle for, "What comes, will come. There isn't much I can do about it." You often carry or say the mantra "Everything happens for a reason." Now this statement can be a very powerful statement. However, more often than not this statement is planted in victimhood. When said in a place of victimhood what it really means is, "What happens, happens and there isn't anything I can do about it so I just accept it."

When your Spiritual Body is playing this dominant role in your life, out of balance with the rest of your four bodies, its place is of great weakness and indifference. This is because when your Spiritual Body isn't balanced by the strengths of the other three bodies, you lack the strength or motivation to act upon or do anything to affect change in your life. You get stuck in complacency and indifference. When the Spiritual Body is playing the dominant role, you tend to want to just let everything happen and do your best to "roll with the punches." What will be, will be, and you actually give up the very power of creation this Spiritual Body actually gives you. You try and avoid getting too set on anything for fear it may not happen, and you can't bear the idea of being disappointed one more time. You tend you use words and phrases like:

- If only...
- What would that be like?
- I wish...but nothing good happens for me.
- Wouldn't it be nice...?

What happens when your Spiritual Body is in balance:

When your Spiritual Body is in balance with the other three bodies it becomes an extraordinary, powerful creating force for all things in your life. You recognize that all things are created from the Love Energy that permeates the Universe, and if you work in balance with your Emotional, Mental, and Physical Bodies, all things are yours for the asking. "Ask and it shall be given you," which is often quoted in several religious texts. You develop a deep trust and even knowing that the world is yours for the asking. When you're in balance in the Spiritual Body, you recognize that you don't know all things and therefore are not dead set on how to bring your desire and dreams to fruition. You just know that they will come one way or another, and you'll be guided along the way for how to achieve them.

The Emotional Body

Your Emotional Body is often referred to in common lingo as your subconscious mind. This is the place where the sum total of all of your life experiences, circumstances, and situations have been stored. This is the aspect that makes your soul unique to you and who you are. The Emotional Body is the driving force for all things relating to your current life, reality, and why you are or are not seeing things manifest in your life right now. Your Emotional Body is made from the emotions and belief systems that you've created because of your life experiences.

Think of the Emotional Body this way—it's the driver of the car you call life. As a passenger—which your Spiritual, Mental and Physical Bodies are passengers—you can tell, yell, plead, beg, and cry for the driver, the Emotional Body, to change course, but you can't actually force the driver to safely change course.

Let's say growing up you were constantly shushed every time you tried talking. It didn't matter how important what you needed or wanted to say was, you were still shushed. This repetitive experience may have been programmed in your Emotional Body as, "What I have to say doesn't matter and therefore I can never say what I'm thinking or feeling." As an adult you realize you never speak up for yourself and it drives you nuts.

You try all the time to *finally* muster up the courage to speak your mind and say what you feel, but you just cannot. There is a reason this doesn't change. Your Mind, or Mental Body, recognizes this pattern in your life but isn't in the driver's seat and therefore cannot force a change in course. You must first heal the emotions and beliefs stored in your Emotional Body, and then your Mental Body will finally have the freedom to do what it desires, which in this example is to speak up for yourself.

Indicators that your Emotional Body is your dominant body:

When your Emotional Body is the dominant body, controlling the majority of your life, everything you experience seems random, disjointed, and even chaotic. You're fine, happy, loving, and easy going one moment, only to be irrational, upset, depressed, and overwhelmed in the next. You experience constant highs and lows in your life and you cling to the "good moments" in hopes that this time these feelings will finally last. You react negatively more often than you do positively and you constantly feel like you're helpless. You feel like you're on an emotional rollercoaster that is never going to stop. You desperately crave to be happy-go-lucky and always thinking life is good, but what you feel is just so real that it just isn't realistic to behave that way. You care deeply for others and find yourself becoming fast friends with people you just meet.

However, you fear being too close because you've got so much to deal with in your own life that it's hard to understand how you can help another and be there for them. Or in the other extreme, you have lots of friends and you live at the center of all their drama and lives. You get lost in their lives and problems in a subconscious attempt to ignore your problems. You make the majority of your decisions based on how you feel, and if you feel fear or nervousness you take that as a "no" to whatever you were inquiring about. As a result, you often find yourself frustrated. You can't ever seem to get anywhere because you're always getting "no" for an answer.

What happens when your Emotional Body is in balance:

When your Emotional Body is in balance with your other three bodies, you're much more capable of living your life from a place of compassion and love for yourself and others. Decisions are made by consulting all aspects of you, and as a result you see that your decisions continuously lead you to achieve your dream and goals. You often feel at peace and fulfilled. You aren't dead set on the "how" to achieve your dreams and desires, preventing you from being disappointed or bitter when things don't go as planned. Rather, you're able to quickly regroup, go within, and begin consulting with all of your being about how best to achieve your goals and quickly put a new plan in place. When your Emotional Body is in balance, you tend to feel a lot of peace and joy knowing that whatever arises in your life can be healed, and there are solutions for all things.

The Mental Body

Now we're onto your Mental Body. This is often referred to as the conscious mind. In this body, a majority of your decisions are made and also a lot of your struggles are recognized. You make observations about your life from this body, and it's where you often determine whether or not you're happy with your current circumstances. This is where your *perception* of life is manifested. The combination of the emotions and beliefs in the Emotional Body come together in this, the Mental Body, to create your perceptions.

Perception is the voice that speaks very dominantly from this body. If you had fallen out of a tree as a child, the emotions and beliefs created from the experience could be:

Emotion – Heights are scary and unsafe.
Belief – I will fall any time I'm too high off the ground.
Resulting Perception – This example results in your perception of the world being something like, "I don't climb trees or stand on high ledges because they're always dangerous and I'll get hurt."

The Mental Body is where life observation takes place, and if it isn't in balance with the other three bodies, it can lead to making very biased and slanted decisions *unknowingly*. The Mental Body is often the first responder to anything that happens in life and also the one where many decisions are made, especially using logic. Now logic is a beautiful thing, however, logic doesn't incorporate a broader, unbiased perception of the world. It's built on facts, or perceived facts, and therefore lacks the input from the Spiritual Body, or intuition, to make decisions from a place of wholeness, considering all options. The Mental Body on its own says, "This is what I see so this is what must be," without taking into account what one is feeling emotionally, physically or intuitively, which come from the Emotional, Physical and Spiritual Bodies.

Indicators that your Mental Body is dominant:

If you grew up having very little spiritual connection, feeling unloved or undervalued, or with parents or guardians who were rather detached from emotion or connection with you, then it's very likely you've been forced to make your Mental Body the dominant decision maker and ruler of your life. You tend to be very judgmental and critical of yourself and others. Perfection is the expectation and you must point out when you or others are falling short of the expectations. You criticize yourself and others for perceived failures—it may even feel like your duty. You make decisions very logically and you want the proof and facts laid out in black and white. You take time to consider the facts as you see them and then very logically create a plan of attack to move through the problem, often even resorting to bulldozing your way through. You take things head on and often resort to force or manipulation to bring about solutions because you feel, "If anything is going to change, then damn it, I'm the only one who can make it happen!"

You tend to be no-nonsense and matter of fact in all approaches to life. Emotional responses in others cause you to feel extremely uncomfortable, and you may tend to feel it's used as a form of manipulation. You care for only a few select people and as a general rule keep most people at a distance. People may have the perception that you're a jerk, calloused, non-feeling and even intimidating.

Relationships tend to have a business feel and are about what each person can get out of the relationship. If at any point you're no longer getting anything out of the relationship, it may be easy for you to walk away or move on. You don't take time for the froufrou, feel good stuff because realistically, at the end of the day, those things won't get anything done or make things happen. You may look at challenges as an opportunity to conquer them and therefore tend to respond with an exactness and callousness that brings about a swift solution or resolve.

What happens when your Mental Body is in balance:

Your Mental Body is truly an extraordinary blessing. It serves as the central hub of communication between all four of your bodies and is the place within you that executes any actions in life. When your Mental Body is in balance with the other three bodies, you're able to take into consideration the facts while simultaneously consulting with how you feel emotionally, what you're hearing from your intuition (or Higher Power), and also how your body is feeling.

This collaborative approach allows you to much more quickly and easily make decisions from a place of wholeness resulting in you achieving greater success, healing, and fulfillment much quicker than anticipated or even hoped for. The Mental Body, when in balance, allows you to be critiqued without feeling judgment or shame because it recognizes that positive critique leads to growth and change. It takes input from others in stride without letting the resulting insight crush its ego or confidence. When in balance, your Mental Body looks forward to feedback and input from the world and others because it affords you an opportunity for growth and change in your life.

When you bring your Mental Body into alignment with your Spiritual, Emotional and Physical Bodies, it's truly like magic happens! You no longer live your life from a place of conflict riddled with guilt, regret, and shame over past decisions or events. You open yourself up to embrace the Love Energy from the Universe, yourself, and those around you, allowing you to flow much more easily in life, while still remaining extremely successful and fulfilled. Your Mental Body, when in balance, opens the doorway for rapid healing and growth because it's no longer about what you know but what you allow yourself to experience that creates the success and solutions you seek in your life.

The Physical Body

The Physical Body is literally your physical body, but it's also the physical world that surrounds you. Our Physical Body is the road map and key to understanding ourselves. It's the place where things are finally manifested. As a result it allows you the opportunity to see what's happening in your life and take cues from it to create healing and change. For example, if you realize you're constantly experiencing a shortage of financial means, this isn't happening because God chose to punish you. It continues happening because there's something in your Emotional Body that resonates with this financial struggle. You inquire within by having your brain, or Mental Body, ask your Spiritual Body, or intuition, what emotions and beliefs in your Emotional Body are manifesting this Physical experience. When you receive your answer, you will then go about healing it.

Our Physical Body is truly one of our greatest blessings! Your Physical body continually provides you a real-time map of your life and allows you to see what is or isn't enabling the Love Energy of our Universe and Creator to flow through there. When you experience illness, pain, aches, hurtful relationships, financial struggle, self-judgment or hatred, your Physical Body and realm gives you huge, blaring clues as to what needs to be healed in your Emotional Body. Then your Emotional Body, the driver of your life, will change course allowing you to have different experiences flow into you. When you have knee pain, there could very realistically be an injury there that is creating the knee pain.

However, the weakness or lack of nutrients in the body that allowed that injury to occur in the first place happened because somewhere, stored in you, were emotions and beliefs that resonated with that injury. For example, the knees typically emotionally tie to the stability and strength we feel in moving forward with life and embracing one's purpose and mission. Like the knees, every single part of your body has a specific aspect of your emotions and belief systems that is stored there. It's absolutely fascinating when you start realizing the emotional connections among all aspects of your life!

Indicators that your Physical Body is dominant:

When your Physical Body plays the dominant role over all the rest of your bodies, you tend to struggle a lot with physical addictions. Whether with food, drugs, alcohol, sex, or anything else, any kind of physical addiction is a really good indicator that you're living primarily in this body. You're driven by what *feels* good in the moment regardless of what the consequences may be later. You have tendency to feel a lot of emptiness and therefore are often looking for things outside of yourself to try and fill that emptiness. You tend to be a glutton for most things in life and typically operate from the mindset where more is always better, regardless of what it is. You tend to have a lot of self-hate or even a very low self-esteem. You may even participate in self-destructive behaviors such as self-harm.

There are two extremes that result from a person living with their Physical Body as the dominant body. The first is from a place of complete and total weakness. You're constantly taken advantage of and have little or no ability to speak up for yourself. You're out of control in your body and may have a tendency to be overweight or even obese. Food or other vices seem completely impossible to rid yourself of. No matter how much you want to change, you feel completely helpless and hopeless because you're so controlled by things outside of you that you don't have the strength to stand up and say, "Enough!" You wallow in shame and disappointment and see very little value within yourself. You go from one "feel-good fix" to the next hoping to drown out the emptiness and lack of fulfillment you feel.

The other extreme when your Physical Body is your dominant operating body is strength and lots of it! You're driven by your own self-power. You may have an *addiction* to fitness and eating healthy and hold yourself to an extreme standard of perfection in your physical endeavors. You're strong, independent, and you don't listen to anyone. You know what's best for you and no one can tell you otherwise. You have an incredible amount of self-control and often deny yourself any number of things. You crave control and order, and you'll do whatever it takes to have that. You're the master of your body and life and have an attitude of, "Life. Will. Obey. Me."

There's no time to rest or relax because those things make you lazy and cause you to fail. You hold a great deal of self-judgment and are often extremely critical. You take no time to enjoy victories or accomplishments because you're already focused on what comes next. You tend to be uptight, overbearing, and cynical. You fear failure and therefore stay in an almost constant motion in an attempt to avoid failure. Rest and relaxation are luxuries you can't afford because they will cause you to fail.

What Happens when your Physical Body is in balance:

When your Physical Body is in balance, you're able to honor your feelings but not be controlled by them. You can draw upon the strengths of your other three bodies to make *wholesome* decisions in your life that are motivated by love. You have a good relationship with yourself and know when your body needs something. You also pay attention to your intuition to know what that is. You accept advice from others without feeling forced to accept or be angered and indignant by it. This is possible because you recognize that you don't have to accept everything someone says but rather you can glean the truths from their statements that resonate with you. Input from others is seen as an opportunity to grow rather than viewed as them tearing you down and criticizing you. You're able to maintain a healthy balance between being focused on the future and taking time to enjoy the present. You're motivated to work with your Physical Body and see the strength and gifts it possesses while still taking time to rest and relax and enjoy life.

The Four Bodies in Balance

The four bodies—the Spiritual Body, Emotional Body, Mental Body and Physical Body—play a powerful role in not only understanding your life but also in *you* being the Creator of your life. When you think of the four bodies, you can liken it to the Russian nesting dolls that have a doll within a doll.

The smallest doll at the center is your Physical Body and physical world. Encompassing that doll is your Mental Body. Then comes the next doll, the Emotional Body, which encompasses your Mental and Physical bodies. Finally encompassing all three of those bodies in the biggest doll of them all is the Spiritual Body. Your Spiritual Body though is without limits. As such, it has access to all resources in the Universe whether you seek answers, abundance, health, love, relationships, or so many others. This Spiritual Body is infinite and where all *your* truth lies.

The Emotional Body, otherwise referred to as the subconscious mind, acts as the gatekeeper to all things. If your emotions and beliefs, which reside in this Emotional Body, or doll, say you have to be in hurtful relationships, then your Emotional Body places a filter between your Physical Body and your Spiritual Body (the provider of all things), only allowing you to have relationships that fit the mold of those emotions and beliefs that manifest within your physical realm.

To see a visual demonstration of how your four bodies work with one another, go to

http://www.joannaashley.com/embracing-your-truth/

and access chapter 2 resources.

3
What's True for You, Is True for You

Now that you have a clearer understanding of your being and how you function, let's apply this knowledge to embrace your truth. The journey to embrace your truth is often called the journey within and requires an earnest willingness to push through negative emotions like hate, fear, and judgment. Your journey within is a search for an inner truth that resounds fiercely without compromise or fear of rejection from anyone. This is what living a life of authenticity is all about. It's a genuine life that fully accepts the imperfections of humanity we all possess and persists with compassion in spite of transgressions, rejection, or hate. To live what's true for you means expressing an authentic life based on what *you know is right* for you.

When you live your truth, you can develop the ability to confidently use your voice, create healthy boundaries for yourself and with others, and honor your own happiness. Living your life's purpose involves a willingness to use compassion and courage with yourself, your relationships, your career or business, and anything you choose to create.

We create our days filled with work, errands, caring for others, and doing what's necessary to survive. Therefore, it's easy to get caught up in our responsibilities. In a blink we can forget to check in with ourselves to find what we truly want and need. Time passes quickly and before we know it, we're off to bed for the night only to start another day.

In your daily activities, do you take time for yourself? Or are you on automatic pilot with little consideration for your personal goals and desires? Do you set aside time to be in the present moment with yourself so you can hear your voice? If you haven't set aside time up to this point in your life, that's okay. However, if you're ready to reflect, live authentically, and create your life on your own terms—you're in the right place *now*.

Authentically Living Your Truth

Living your truth authentically is a journey of self-discovery and a purposeful act on your part every day. Authenticity can manifest different things for you like health, money, homes, cars, a business, or even better relationships. Whatever manifests from living your truth authentically, the bottom line is the same—it's all about coming to a real place within you. Living your truth allows your voice to rise above the noise of the day-to-day and advocates the best path for you. It's also about surrendering to that still, quiet voice within that has answers and the truth which is relevant to your questions and circumstances. There are no boundaries or shortcomings within you; it's simply trusting you have what you need at any moment. Living your truth only requires you to let go of past shame, guilt, and resentments. It requires you to live in the moment free of judgment or negativity.

Live in the Moment

In *The Power of Now: A Guide to Spiritual Enlightenment*, author Eckhart Tolle states, "*Die to the past every moment. You don't need it. Only refer to it when it's absolutely relevant to the present. Feel the power of this moment and the fullness of Being. Feel your presence.*"

Every waking moment we're bombarded with a myriad of news events, disasters, bits of information, and we are invited to worry about the future with thoughts like, "Have I saved enough money for retirement?" Headlines highlight rumors of war, arrests for crimes, insider trading, and who the stars are dating this week. Rarely are we invited to be present *now* and really live in the moment. Live in the now.

We're rushed through our day. If you have a fleeting moment to think about it, you may consider living in the moment. But with our busy schedules, who has time for such frivolity? However, it's vital to your happiness to make the time, feel the present, and embrace your being wholly. To experience the present, here is a quick exercise to help you focus on living in the *now*.

Take a deep breath just for a minute or two and suspend all your thoughts about what you must and should do for today, next week, the month or the entire year. Observe present time by feeling your environment—the chair you sit upon, your feet on the floor, the sounds of the room and any other sense you can gather. Are you here yet? Right here in the present you're perfectly made. Here in the present, you have everything you need for your journey through life including the right questions and the answers. Should anything contradict this truth, push it away.

Your truth exists without any fear or prejudice. It's not based on your past, and it supports you and your ability to express it wholly. If you sense any anxiety while doing this, take a moment and ask yourself, without thinking of an answer, "What does it feel like to feel love and peace in this moment?" In this space, where you're at right now, you can create and design your life and your results based on what's true for you. The power of living in the now doesn't rely on your past, nor is it dependent upon your future. Actually, it's here in this moment without judgment, fear, anxiety, or any negativity at all. Being here now allows you to experience the acceptance of others, your encounters, and what the moment offers you.

Not Everything Is Black and White

The beliefs you carry on your journey and the values you hold are often derived from the rules given by our family, friends, communities, churches and religions, and the thoughts expressed through those who surround us in our immediate environment. We're taught how we should see the world, how things ought to be, and, if we try to express anything contrary to this, we're often warned and sometimes punished.

Many religions give such strict structures that questioning anything they teach is looked down upon and discouraged. I don't feel the majority of the people in religious leadership positions intend to restrict or stunt a person's growth and evolution, but they see following the rules so strictly as a way to stay safe and be blessed. I believe the strict guidelines that are given, which often seem beyond reproach, cause people to live in a place of autopilot, never stopping to think for themselves how they *feel* about the rules and what's taught.

You may be one of many who have consciously delved into how you feel about the rules and guidelines of your respective beliefs and religion and found peace there. This is fantastic. It shows a conscious participation, alignment and acceptance, which allows you to live much more fully and completely in those beliefs. Others have consciously inquired within about their current beliefs only to find much is lacking, but they are faced with fear, ridicule, and chagrin should they desire to change.

Oftentimes the truths we live by haven't even consciously been told to us. Rather they're created from the experiences we encounter through life. Unfortunately many of us had a great deal of our truths borne from well-meaning adults who wanted to force us to behave in accordance with socially acceptable standards, while others may have experienced abuse of one kind or another. Abuse is never easy to endure, especially as children, because we're dependent upon our parents, relatives, and peers to help us survive and grow. Often when such things are experienced as children and teenagers, we don't even realize the impact and implications they have on our adult lives.

An example of this, say a person was sexually abused as a child and may have even repressed the memories. As an adult, they find themselves bored with sex or intimacy and find it hard to engage their significant other in such a way that they have just written off sex and intimacy as "not their thing." This is an example of something stored in the Emotional Body affecting the Physical Body because of the perception held in the Mental Body. Once you can heal and clear the emotions and beliefs stored in the Emotional Body, the Mental perception changes, resulting in a change in the Physical Body and the person's desire to have intimacy and sex with their significant other. It's all a chain of events. Heal the beginning cause and you heal the end result.

If you've survived abuse, then I'm sure you've learned how to tread lightly when it comes to your needs and wants because having an outspoken voice or an opinion opens the door to punishment. As a result, you probably learned to live in silence because you were taught you didn't matter. In homes where invalidation and unkindness lurk, emotional and physical safety are absent. If you grew up in a home where your opinion had little value, it's possible, actually likely, for you to carry this negative belief into adulthood.

John J. Lemoncelli, author of *Healing from Childhood Abuse: Understanding the Effects, Taking Control to Recover*, writes, *Abuse destroys the ability of the victims to trust themselves and others. Some victims have carried these burdens their entire lives because they couldn't share the shame, the guilt, and the tremendous responsibility they carried for what happened to them.*

Not just from abuse, but if our wants and needs are continually rejected as invalid, we learn well the art of masking our feelings, our thoughts, and what we want. More importantly, we don't know how to give ourselves permission to create life on our own terms.

We become emotionally stunted because we're unable to heal our own pain. Therefore, we're consumed with pleasing others all the time to avoid feelings of loss or rejection. While we endlessly concern ourselves with the needs of others, we're unable to truly live our purpose. The evidence of abuse, whether it's physical, sexual, psychological, or spiritual, can manifest in many ways. Behaviors like alcoholism, abusing others, promiscuity, withdrawal from life, and even having many illnesses are common.

Living Life with Your Beliefs

Spiritual and religious freedom is the right of every person on this planet regardless of the country you reside in or the rules you live by. We have the inalienable right to believe in God, a Higher Power, Mother Earth, Spirit, or nothing at all because we're unique and have individual perspectives and viewpoints. I've learned each person has their own personal truth which has many paths, each unique to that person and their journey through life. A person's truth can be derived from the foundations laid in their religious upbringing, and their truths may stem from life experiences that cause them to see the world differently.

Whatever you believe today is the sum result of all your experiences to date in your life. The reality, though, is a great deal of your beliefs are built on false perceptions, half-truths, and the emotions you've stored from all your life experiences.

You have the divine right to discover and live your own truth with unhindered pursuit. The beauty of being in this place where you're only responsible for living your own truth is *the need to be right* goes away. In this journey it's not about proving others wrong or even having to make everyone see the world as you do, it's about coming to a place of peace where you're happy, confident, and thriving in your own life because your rules are finally working for you. You can confidently have conversations with others because you no longer fear being proven wrong or that you must make others see things your way.

Rather, you have conversations where you can focus on listening and sincerely replying in thoughtful ways. It has been amazing to see how much my conversations have changed since I found my truth. I hear so much more clearly what others are saying because I'm standing in a place of love with them, instead of standing against them afraid I will have to prove myself and make them see things my way. Embracing your truth allows you stand with others in love always, because you *know* who you are and are confident in who you are.

Think of it this way. You've been looking at buying a new car for ages. You've researched, driven, smelled, felt, and touched countless cars in your quest for exactly the right one. Now you're purchasing this dream car of yours, and it's a Chevrolet Camaro with all the extras. You sign the papers and hop in to take your new beauty home. On the way home though you decide to stop by and show your friend your new car. Imagine pulling up in front of your friend's house and getting out of your car just in time to see your friend running toward you from the house, mad as can be. He stops just on the other side of the car from you and proceeds to yell at you and tell you how you've bought the wrong car—this is the stupidest decision of your life, how dare do something so hurtful and go against him—he rants and raves and finally tells you were supposed to actually buy the new Ford Mustang because that's *his* favorite car. Can you imagine?

This unfortunately happens quite often in our world. We make life decisions based upon what we're thinking and feeling as well as what resonates most with us. Then if what we have chosen goes against what another person would do, they take it personally and tell us we're ruining their life.

The whole point of living *your* truth is realizing each of us is unique and different things will work for each of us. Our focus should not be on how differently we do things, but rather how we support others to do something that makes them happy and makes their lives work better. In this scenario, *knowing* your truth and standing in love would allow you to not be offended by your friend and rather to respond to his outburst with compassion. You could reply with something like, "I'm so sorry you're so upset about my choice because you wanted a different car. What can we do to help *you* get the car of *your* dreams?" Immediately you've diffused the situation and opened up the flow of Love Energy to bring a solution to the apparent hurt your friend is feeling.

This kind of self-love and knowing your truth allows you to respond with understanding, rather than more hurt when someone does or says something that's hurtful or offensive. How cool is that? You never have to be offended again.

In my own life I've gone through this phase of complete transformation of my beliefs. I was raised in an extremely religious, Christian home. My parents did the absolute best that they could to teach me the rules and "laws" of our religion in hopes I could live a happy and fulfilling life safely because of the safety those rules and laws could afford me. They did the absolute best they could and wanted me to be happy.

At eighteen, as a young adult, I fasted, prayed, and studied my heart out to discover this religion and its beliefs did in fact resonate with me and my soul. I found great peace and carried on in my practice of this religion. Fast forward a few years, and at twenty-two I was having a crisis of faith. I was trying to maintain and live all the rules of this religion, but I couldn't make them work in my life. What I wanted to achieve and where I was drawn required me to see the world in a drastically different way.

I hit rock bottom spiritually. The wars between my head and heart consumed everything, and I felt like I was being splintered and torn from within, like at any moment my head might physically explode because of the discontent and nonstop warring happening inside me. In a desperate attempt to experience peace and finally silence the war in my head, I made a rash decision and chose atheism. It afforded me the silence I so desperately craved—no wars, no fighting voices claiming one was right over the other, just sweet silence. If there wasn't anything spiritual and no God, then neither side could say much. I mentally stuck my tongue out and said, "Neener, neener!" to both the religious (head) and spiritual (heart) sides of me that were warring. Neither of them could say anything in this place.

My choice for atheism only lasted three days though as the silence I experienced in that place possessed nothing more than silence. I was devoid of emotion or connection with anything in this place. It was difficult to endure but necessary for my growth. After two days I started doubting my decision, and by the third day I could no longer ignore the fact that this place didn't bring me any peace either. So, I went back to the drawing board.

Intuitively I knew there was a Creator, a Higher Power, and we're all spiritual beings. But, I didn't possess any knowledge or information to lean on. My mind and heart were in a spiritual tug-of-war battle. My spirit knew there was another way, a higher purpose and a truth to live by. However, my mind was still stuck in the old way of thinking that came straight from my upbringing. I struggled to shed the traditional precepts I was raised with and adopt a completely new set of beliefs.

In my mind I came to this room where there were tables upon tables completely covered and piled with stuff and the tables went on for miles in either direction. On the other side of the table stood my Creator, God if you will. I looked at my Creator and fell to my knees and from my tormented heart cried, "Please, take *everything* away from me that isn't truth, I don't know what's true anymore."

In an instant all the tables and everything on them disappeared. What remained was one single, solitary table standing between me and my Creator with nothing on it. My Creator held his arms out to me and I ran to be by his side. While embracing me in a hug, he said, "Now we can build your truth together." I made my decision in that moment. I chose to follow the voice within me urging me forward. I trusted I was making the right move *for me* and in the end, I'd be okay.

A paradigm shift occurred and ignited a passion within me to seek and live my truth with no shame and no regrets.

What happened in that moment was I left the religion of my upbringing and I embraced *my truth*. This wasn't to say anyone had to follow me or believe what I did. In fact I realized I could reside perfectly in this place of my new truth while wholeheartedly loving and supporting my family members who remained in their place of truth within their religion.

It was no longer a game of who was right and who was wrong. It was about each of us embracing what felt true and brought love, peace, joy, healing and success in our lives. If our truths looked drastically different, it didn't matter because we could still love and support each other in our respective places of fulfillment.

Discovering Your Truth

> *I want to challenge you today to step outside of your comfort zone. You've so much incredible potential on the inside. God has put gifts and talents in you that you probably don't know anything about.*
> —Joel Osteen

This may be a new journey for you, and as you discover your own truth, you may experience the joy of freedom and doing something for yourself you've never done before. This journey is no longer about who is right or wrong. It's about what's best and true for each of us individually and having confidence and love in that new truth. The journey within is a quiet but turbulent road, filled with new discoveries and a recovery of lost information. Your experiences have prepared you to go beneath the surface and dig for the hidden treasure within called *you*.

I know inside you reside answers to the many questions you have about yourself, your purpose, and how to create the life you truly want to live. You're unique and your view of the world and your purpose is important and unlike any other. If you're struggling with doubt, fear, anxiety, or anger, you can turn this around and begin your personal journey to discover your own truth. Healing past hurts and opening the door to compassion and joy are within you.

The voyage on the road to living your truth will open the door to many insights about you. Recognizing your truth may begin as a bumpy road but steadily will provide many "ah-ha" moments of peace, excitement, and certainty. When you find what's true for you, you'll finally discover an astonishing calmness because your authentic voice is finally allowed to speak. This may be the first time you're permitted such freedom of expression and belief. I've provided tools along the way to help you become more self-aware. You will gain the self-knowledge necessary to traverse on your personal adventure.

Something I want to stress in this moment is that embracing your truth isn't a journey with a destination. You'll build a good foundation to move forward; however, the beauty of this journey is you're continually learning, growing, and changing and as a result so will your truth. What you may embrace completely as truth in this moment may look completely different three years from now because of the growth and knowledge you've gained. The way you're guided in your truth is by communicating with yourself and following the path that resonates with allowing the abundant flow of Love Energy.

Tool Two: Exploring What's True for You

A great way to determine if you're living in your truth is to go through this checklist and see how many you can answer "yes."

1. Do you feel loved by yourself, others, and most importantly by your Higher Power?
2. Are you experiencing moments of joy at least once a day?
3. Do you experience a moment of peace at least once a day?
4. Is your body healthy and free from dis-ease, aches, pains or injuries or currently being healed of these things?
5. Do you have abundance flowing into your life? Are your needs continuously met, and it's not a struggle to make ends meet?

If you can answer "yes" to all five of these questions that is an excellent indicator you're well on the path of *your truth*.

Congratulations!

However, if you couldn't confidently answer, "yes," to all these questions, it's a good indicator you're still living to some degree by others' truths.

This next part of the tool is to help you begin gleaning insight from your Creator and the Universe about *your truth*. These questions are more than your everyday questions. They come with an extraordinary amount of power and the capacity to help you shift and learn in ways you haven't even considered.

When you ask this question below, your body will typically respond in one of two ways:

1. If you have a feeling of anxiety or a lack of ease, it's an indicator something isn't your truth.
2. If your response is a feeling of peace and calm, then chances are this is your truth.

Question:

"Disregarding my bias and opinions, what does it feel like to have God's truth and perspective on _____?"

For example, "Disregarding my bias and opinions, what does it feel like to have God's truth and perspective on whether I'm really supposed to have abundance and prosperity?"

Or, "Disregarding my bias and opinions, what does it feel like to have God's truth and perspective whether my life is supposed to be filled with love?"

Always ask the question framed in a positive way. Ask about what you want to create in your life rather than what you don't want in your life.

This first part of the journey can feel extremely intimidating and overwhelming. There are so many questions, and the "how to do this" can feel like it will squash you. I have a mini coaching session and additional tools available at my website to help you develop this tool. You can access them at

http://www.joannaashley.com/embracing-your-truth/

and go to chapter 3 resources.

I want to be here to support and help you embrace your truth. This online community and the tools are all about you. The first step to discovering *your* truth is becoming conscious of your thoughts.

4
Your Emotions and Beliefs Create the Rules You Live By

The emotions you carry combined with your beliefs create how you perceive the world around you which results in the current rules you accept as truth. Simply put:

Emotions + Belief = Perception

Seeing this in relation to your four bodies, your Emotional Body creates your perception of reality. As a result, your emotions and belief systems determine the rules and truths you live by throughout your life. Emotions and beliefs have the power to create your reality, and the reality you create is perceived and reinforced by the experiences you have. Put simply, your emotions and beliefs are the boss. Your perceptions are what create your reality. Whatever you believe to be true is true whether it's based on factual information or not. You have the power to create experiences by cleaning up the emotions and belief systems you rely on for your truth.

Your emotions and beliefs so strongly persuade your perception, which is why in the tool in the last chapter the question says, "Disregarding my bias and opinions..." This phrase is energetically shifting your Emotional Body from being the driver of your perception and putting your Spiritual Body, with its infinite connection with your Creator in the driver seat using all of the perspective and truth from your Creator to give you guidance according to your divine truth.

Good Feelings and Thoughts Create a Good Reality

Everything is energy and that's all there is to it. Match the frequency of the reality you want and you cannot help but get that reality. It can be no other way. This isn't philosophy. This is physics.

—Bashar

For instance, if your emotions and beliefs say you're not good enough, you'll create relationships with others reinforcing this perception where you're judged as "not enough." You'll manifest outcomes like poor income and constant struggle, and it will be difficult to achieve true satisfaction in your life. This is a low-level game because you've been created to accomplish great things.

The same is true if you exude confidence and joy—you're operating on a high-energy frequency that attracts the same emotions and thought patterns. This frequency creates stability, better relationships, more solutions, and better opportunities. Fear is an emotional stranglehold that deconstructs the good thoughts and feelings we have and the experiences we manifest.

Fear has the power to distort your reality, cause confusion, and sap the hope from you if you're driven by it. The purpose of fear is to stop you from creating, flourishing, and finding confidence in your own existence and that of others. Its purpose is to cut off the flow of Love Energy in your life. Left unchecked, fear eventually can cause you to dive straight into a state of apathy. Fear causes worries about money, loved ones, or even how you'll get your basic necessities met. It also causes anxiety about the future and the past. Fear stops the flow of peace through a physical response like rapid heartbeat, sweaty palms, irrational nervousness, and more.

In order to get back into a place where the Love Energy of our Creator and Universe is allowed to flow, we must be able to first *feel* something good. If you're riddled with anger, hurt, betrayal, bitterness, disappointment, or any other set of fear-based emotions, you'll continue manifesting circumstance in which these feelings are perpetuated. Many people get caught in this cycle because they say things like, "I won't be angry anymore when I have money," or, "When I'm better I'll be happy."

Their current state of existence and the potential for it to change is placed in the control of some future event that may or may not happen. What's coming cannot be promised or guaranteed, so it's up to us to *choose* to feel something in this present moment regardless whether something does or does not change.

Many people, and possibly even you as well, are dealing with a lot of financial struggle. They're overworked, underpaid, unappreciated, and working their guts out in the hope that somehow something will happen to change these situations. I'll use finances as an example. Dad comes home from another ridiculously long day and he's angry, worn out, and exhausted. His daughter comes running into the living room excited to greet her dad. On the way to him she trips, knocks over the end table and breaks the lamp. She gets up and is sorry, but it's too late. Dad is running over to her, picks her up, and proceeds to bend her over his knee and spank her for breaking the lamp. Then he sends her crying to her room without dinner. Later the father feels awful for his actions, but he justifies them with something like, "Well, things will be better when we finally get this financial situation figured out."

So how long will this cycle last?

How many times will he come home and spank his daughter for her mistakes? At the root, he's actually angry at himself and his family's predicament. But his daughter is a channel for that anger, and every time it happens, he promises he will be a better dad and treat her better when finances change. If it never happens, his daughter will spend her whole life into adulthood bearing the brunt of his self-anger and self-disappointment because things never changed.

However, he could decide to change the way he feels right then and there regardless of the financial situation. He could take five minutes before he walks in the door from work to let go of the worry and get lost in feeling and thinking about his blessings. He could feel how much he loves his daughter and is grateful for her. He could focus on how much he loves his wife, and regardless of the few dollars they have in their checking account, she still loves him and cares for him. He has a roof over his family's head, and for one more day he was able to provide money for them to live on.

If he focused his attention on the blessings he does have, he would immediately create a shift in his feelings to resonate with bringing more blessings to be grateful for—eventually causing his feelings and beliefs to resonate with a solution for the financial issues.

Changing your feelings and thoughts is as simple as doing a self-evaluation to determine if they resonate with the outcome you desire. In this example the dad perceives he'll be happy when he has money. Well, what would happen if he felt that happiness for himself right now instead of feeling anger! Choosing to change how we feel is a conscious choice and one that requires us to look at all situations from the bigger picture, rather than just what's happening in the now.

Tool Three: Create Your Reality through Your Emotions and Beliefs

The tool I provide here is intended to help you begin getting comfortable with looking at your life through a lens of observation, question, and discovery so you can begin choosing your feelings and thoughts rather than be ruled by them. The focus is to help you gently transition out of living on autopilot and instead live a life where you're proactive and in your place as the Creator of your life.

I have a mini coaching session available at

http://www.joannaashley.com/embracing-your-truth/

Go to chapter 4 resources.

The idea of this coaching session is to help answer many of the common questions that come with the transition and to help you feel encouraged and empowered to begin your journey.

Much like in the previous tools, this tool again is a series of questions I want you take time to ask and then receive an answer from within. When you're in a cycle of fear-based emotions, as described previously, you cannot force yourself to feel something different.

Rather you must open a doorway to feel something different.

1. When you're feeling something unpleasant, I want you to first ask yourself, "Does this feeling resonate with the outcome I desire?" For example: If you're angry about your current money situation, would you still feel angry when your money situation is resolved?
2. Next I want you to ask yourself, "If I was exactly where I wanted to be, what would I be feeling?" For example: If you had all of your finances resolved you could potentially feel joy, peace, comfortable rest and much excitement at the possibilities.
3. After you realize how you would feel if all was as you wished it to be, ask yourself this question, not thinking of an answer. Just let the question permeate through you. "What does it feel like to feel these love-based emotions and feelings regardless of my current circumstances?" Then take a moment to feel those good feelings settle into your being.

You can do this exercise anytime and anywhere. It's so incredibly powerful to help you quickly shift the course of your life and bring you to a place of harmony with the outcome you desire. By choosing to do this exercise, you are literally opening the flood gates of Love Energy to flow into your life and bring you more love and abundance.

Karen's Story as told by her.

To tell this story I must give pieces from my background. Born and raised in a religious family that had strong beliefs in God and Jesus Christ, I felt I must have been a sinner all my life as I was sexually molested from the time I was a small girl. I had a deep and strong belief that there was a God and Jesus Christ was my savior, but there was a distance between us I didn't know how to bridge. So I was strong and determined this wouldn't happen to my children.

Fast forward to the year 2007 when I learned devastating news. For three years while I was caring for my extremely sick son, who almost died, my other children were raped, molested, and sodomized while in the care of family members. To say I was shocked and distraught was an understatement. So I did the only thing I could–I packed up my family and ran away.

I tried to find God and my Savior to help heal my family and me. After meeting with a religious leader who encouraged me to forgive and move on, I did my best to follow his advice. However, I found it difficult, even nearly impossible. But I pressed on and did the best I could to follow that guidance.

Three years later after much therapy and lots of prayer, I thought we were doing really well. Then I met and got to know JoAnna Ashley. I believe meeting her was a miracle from God. She helped me learn how to change my energy and beliefs and therefore change my life for the better. She taught me to connect with my spirit and as a result finally bridge the distance to God and my

Savior Jesus Christ. She also taught me how to reach out and teach my husband and children to do the same.

Today our world isn't a perfect one, but we now have the tools to handle challenges as they arise. So when issues like anger, hurt, and despondency raise their ugly heads, we're able to connect with our spirit and God. As a result it allows us to align and fix the issues from the past abuse in a healthy, wholesome way instead of self-destructing. We realize now healing from the devastation of the abuse begins within us. Therefore we're not waiting on justice or other people to change things before we can have our peace, healing, and wholeness right now.

Here is a recent example of my daughter, Sarah, using the tools JoAnna taught us to heal and change her life. The other night Sarah had an allergic reaction to something she ate. Her face was swelling and tingling and she was having a difficult time breathing. Knowing the tools she was taught, Sarah utilized them and it made a difference, however it still wasn't enough. So she used the knowledge of essential oils she gained from JoAnna and selected a few oils to help her situation. She had me apply the essential oils to her neck and feet to shift her energy and beliefs.

In about twenty minutes, all Sarah's symptoms were completely healed. The next day, my daughter wanted to completely heal her allergy. She called JoAnna and asked her to help her fix it because she didn't know how. They worked for just a few minutes together, and the result was her allergy was completely healed. It disappeared and has not re-appeared.

In conclusion this is my truth–JoAnna has opened doorways to healing, protecting, and saving my family I never before imagined possible. I don't know where I'd be now without her guidance and wisdom in my life.

5
Your Body Is A Map

Many people today feel alienated from or at war with their bodies. It's a constant fight to maintain health, and before they know it, they've developed another problem. Others view their bodies as hindrances to what their capable and willing mind would love to do. Often I hear people cursing and even angry towards their bodies because they seem to cause more and more problems. I must be honest here and say when I was nearing the peak of all my illnesses and my body was becoming extremely weak, I felt great anger and hatred towards my body and even toward God. How could my body betray me and how could God let it happen? Everything felt chaotic and without rhyme or reason. I directed my anger and frustration toward my body and God.

This was until I realized my body was actually communicating to me. When I realized my body didn't desire existing in a state of weakness, pain, disease, and illness, my perspective and relationship with my body changed. I began recognizing pain, discomfort, and illnesses such as the common cold or diseases were my body's way of communicating the things I wasn't hearing from my intuition or Spiritual Body. Likewise it's the same for you.

Your body is literally creating a map for you, guiding you to recognize what's being stored in your Emotional Body and needs to be healed. I began learning in each of us there's a common ground where certain emotions are stored in the body. The physical pain, discomfort, or whatever is stored there in your body drawing your attention to what you're holding onto so tightly.

I learned the fibromyalgia I, and many others, suffer with was created from a series of emotional traumas or one huge emotional trauma. For example mine was created from the repeated sexual, physical, and mental abuse I experienced as a child. Others I met who have fibromyalgia had its onset after the sudden unexpected loss of a dear loved one, while for others it developed after a traumatic accident or injury. As I pondered this, I came to understand the creation of fibromyalgia like this—within each of us is this balloon-like emotional core where emotions are sent to be dealt with accordingly. Repeated abuse or one exceptionally traumatic event happens, and there's such a large amount of emotional input sent to the emotional balloon's core. It finally explodes like a bomb, sending emotional shrapnel throughout your entire body. As a result the undiagnosable pain, fatigue, forgetfulness, and a myriad of other symptoms are created causing fibromyalgia.

The good news though is once you address and heal the emotions at the core that caused the bomb to go off in the first place, the body heals itself of the fibromyalgia, which is how I cured mine. I timed back and healed my being and emotions before any of the abuse happened, and I cured myself of the fibromyalgia.

Our bodies are beautiful maps that paint a road to our own self-awareness and healing. It requires us to release our judgment and hurt and step into a place of love and compassion for ourselves and others.

Discovering the Root Cause Will Heal the Body and Soul

As mysterious as it may appear, our bodies are actually trying to speak to us in ways that will grab our attention and encourage us to take action to change some facet of our life. I'll teach you how to speak the language of your body and how to begin healing your body and help others heal their own as well.

The foundational piece to understand what I'm about to teach is our bodies are more than just a physical presence. Our beings are essentially made up of so much more than a physical body.

As a being you are the compilation of your Spiritual Body, Emotional Body, Mental Body as well as your Physical Body as discussed in chapter two. Recognizing and understanding this truth opens the doorway for you to understand how the interaction of one to another creates what you see manifesting in your life, especially in your Physical Body.

I've discovered there's a difference between what's manifesting on one side of the body versus the other. I've found on the right side of the body the majority of the time illnesses, aches or pains are more to do with our own selves and our own struggles. The left side of the body seems to deal with those closest to us in our realm of influence. They can be loved ones, family members, friends, coworkers, team mates, etc.

I want to give you some examples to apply this knowledge on how the right-left split applies. Let's say you're experiencing severe pain on the right side of your neck. It's stiff, sore and you can hardly turn your head due to the pain. In the upcoming chart, the neck rootwise emotionally ties into, "Seeing things differently or from a new perspective."

If the right side of your neck is bothering you, then you can ask yourself, "What do I not want to see differently or from a new perspective?"

If it's the left side of your neck in pain however, I suggest asking yourself, "Who do I want to make see things differently?" Then when you get an answer ask yourself, "Why?"

This becomes an opportunity for growth and development of your self-awareness because now you can grasp how you're seeing the world. You're beginning to discover why you feel so strongly about the situation. It also becomes an opportunity to see if you authentically align with what you desire.

Once you take some time to observe the situation, ask yourself a question like, "What does it feel like to see this situation differently and release my need to control how things are seen?" Don't be surprised to find your neck pain will start going away. In this situation you've utilized the clues from your Physical Body to address a belief stored in your Emotional Body. You recognize the perspective created in your Mental Body may not be in alignment with your goals and greater good. All this is possible when you take the time to inquire of your Spiritual Body, "Why?" Why did you feel and see things the way you did? In this moment you unplugged from your autopilot programming and became an active Creator of your life.

In the following charts I share the potential root emotions that store in various body parts. With each of the root emotions or areas where you're experiencing symptoms, ask questions of yourself like:

- Do I fear this?
- Do I feel confident in this?
- What's bothering me about this?
- What is it I need to change in this area?
- What are the emotions I harbor regarding this?

These inquiring questions help you by tuning into your intuition to bring you greater understanding and direction for yourself.

Emotions of the Skeletal Structure

Body Part	Possible Root Emotional Issue
Feet	Direction of one's life
Ankles	Strength to change the direction of one's life
Knees	Stability felt in regards to one's direction
Hips	Decisions that have already been made
Spine	Support and strength one feels about life
Lower Spine	Foundational support issues such as finances, support from others, things that threaten the very foundation of life
Mid Spine	Ability to bend and move with life circumstances
Upper Spine	Carrying the responsibilities one has in life
Ribs	Ability one feels in expanding and growing with life.
Shoulders	Carrying the weight of burdens and concerns
Arm	Exerting one's power
Elbow	Dealing with your power and adjusting it to deal with new circumstances

Wrist	Flexibility we feel in utilizing our power in different ways
Hand	Actually utilizing one's own power
Thumb	Accepting
Pointer Finger	Pointing at others
Middle Finger	Anger
Ring Finger	Relationships
Pinky Finger	Value – feeling valued or giving value
Neck	Seeing things differently or from a new perspective
Skull	The capacity we feel in dealing with life circumstances

Emotions of the Organs

Organ	Possible Root Emotional Issue	Physical Purpose
Brain	Ability to deal/cope with life and circumstances	The seat of the Mental Body and tool used to form cognitive thought and orchestrate the inner workings of one's body
Ears	The impact of what's being heard or spoken out loud or in one's mind, feeling out of balance or sync with life	Hearing and balance
Eyes	Not liking what one is seeing, unable to create a vision	Seeing – Our visual perception of reality
Nose	Not liking what one is smelling, memory tied to a smell that makes them sick, upset, or repulsed	Smelling – affecting the taste of one's food, the emotion felt in an experience
Sinuses	How fluid one feels in utilizing voice and speaking up for one's self	Help humidify the air we breathe in. Another is that they enhance our voices.
Mouth	Acceptance of Nutrients (spiritual, emotional, mental or physical)	Entrance point for nutrients and sustenance to enter one's body

Tongue	Strength or freedom to speak	Aids in moving food in the mouth, chewing and swallowing
Teeth	The strength one feels to speak	Begin the processes of breaking nutrients down to be utilized
Jaw	The first defender of the body. How strong or capable they feel in defending or protecting themselves	Used for grasping and manipulating food
Throat	Ability to speak up and voice ideas or thoughts	Location of voice-box, tonsils, adenoids, etc.
Thyroid	Maintaining balance in life	The *purpose* of your thyroid gland is to make, store, and release thyroid hormones...If you've too little thyroid hormone in your blood, your body slows down.
Thymus	One's ability to discern truth	The thymus gland is a gland that forms part of the immune system
Esophagus	Accepting the nutrients being provided	Carries food, liquids, and saliva (nutrients) from the mouth to the stomach

Heart	The Love Energy center of the body. Where love is either accepted or rejected	To pump blood (the life giving force) to every facet of the body.
Lungs	Grief, trauma, and hurt from others, releasing the old and embracing the new	Bring oxygen (the good) into the body and to remove carbon dioxide (the bad)
Stomach	Stress and deep-seated worry. Trying to sort through everything that comes	Break down food after feeding and extract the nutrients necessary to the body
Liver	The ability to break up and digest toxins and poisons. Anger, frustration, resentment	Get rid of toxins from the blood
Gallbladder	Intense emotions such as rage, fury, loathing	Collect and store bile from the activities of the liver then release it at the appropriate time into the small intestine.
Spleen	Letting go of the old, not allowing one's life to be cleansed and healed	Responsible for purifying the blood as well as storing blood cells

Pancreas	Non-acceptance or lack of the sweet and good things in life	Make insulin for your body so that it can use sugar, or glucose for energy
Kidneys	Control – feeling a need for control, out of control, wanting control, etc	Filter and reprocess blood (life force)
Adrenal Glands	Pacing one's self and overexertion	Keep your body's reactions to stress in balance so that they're appropriate and not harmful
Urinary Tract	Releasing fear	Includes the kidneys, ureters, bladder, and urethra
Bladder	Deep-seated fear that is harbored for some time	Stores urine, allowing urination to be infrequent and voluntary
Small Intestine	Rejection of the nutrients/blessings being provided	Where much of the digestion and absorption of food takes place
Large Intestine/Colon	Rejection of one's own life force	Absorb water from the remaining indigestible food matter, and then pass useless waste material from the body
Rectum	Holding onto the crap that has happened in life	Temporary storage site for feces

Female Organs	Creative abilities – doubt, fear, reject, hate	Purpose of the reproductive system is to reproduce
Ovaries	Insecurity or doubts over the power or ability to begin something or create something new	Produce female sex hormones resulting in puberty and production of egg cells
Fallopian Tubes	Struggle in letting one release their creative power and gifts	Carry eggs from the ovary to the uterus
Uterus	Rejection of creative power, refusing to accept life's cycles	Nourishes a fetus until birth
Cervix	Allowing the release of one's creative powers	Helps lubricate the vaginal area and provides support to pelvic ligaments
Vagina	Not releasing old patterns, rejection of one's sexual desire or needs, blocking the manifestation of your creations	1: To excrete liquid wastes from the body 2: For sexual interaction 3: Birth of a child.
Ureter	Refusing to release the need to control	Propel urine from the kidneys to the urinary bladder
Urethra	Refusing to release the fear	Connects the urinary bladder to the outside of the body

Male Organs		
Penis	Not releasing old patterns, rejection of one's sexual desire or needs, blocking the manifestation of your creations	Sexual gratification, releasing semen, and the release of urine
Testicles	Insecurity or doubts over the power or ability to begin something or create something new	Responsible for making testosterone, the primary male sex hormone, and for generating sperm
Prostate	Insecurity, doubt or fear over one's ability to nurture self and others	Prostate gland contributes additional fluid to the ejaculate, also the fluids help to nourish the sperm
Urethra – Urine	Refusing to release the fear	Connects the urinary bladder to the outside of the body
Urethra – Semen	Refusing to release one's creations into reality	Acts as a conduit for semen during sexual intercourse
Veins	Stopping or restricting the release of the bad from one's body	Veins carry blood back to the heart
Arteries	Stopping or restricting the acceptance of the good into one's body	Arteries carry blood away from the heart.
Bone	Restricting one's ability to move or shift in an area of life	Provide something for muscles to push against to create movement

Tendons	Feeling a disconnect in striving to move on or move in a new direction	Aid in movement of joints by linking muscle to bone
Ligaments	Not feeling connected in one's ability to move in life	Attaches bone to bone
Joints	Not feeling flexible – look at skeletal structure to hone in with what	Provide flexible connections between your bones
Tissue	Rejecting one's ability to heal and move on. Wanting to disconnect or fracture from one's self	Connective tissue holds bone to bone, holds muscle to bone, attaches tissue to tissue, repairs cuts and tears and various leaks in your circulatory system
Muscle	The strength one feels in moving forward in some aspect of life	Move our skeletal system by stretching and contracting
Cartilage	Overwhelmed with trauma or unexpected events	The body's shock absorber

Healing Our Bodies is a Cooperative Effort

When you utilize the tools above, you're using energy to effect change, essentially doing what's now becoming known as "Energy Work." It's the practice of using one's own energy to create healing and change. The energetic connection between all four bodies affords you the ability to do this.

The practice of energy work and holistic healing is a familiar activity to millions of people, especially in Eastern cultures. It's gradually becoming more commonplace in the West in the last two generations. The evolution of man has increased his understanding of physics and energy which has aided the discovery of how you can heal your body through guided steps to cause changes within and around you. The broad shift in new ideas about our bodies and the power therein has created the holistic movement.

Holistic healing approaches our spirit, emotions, mind and body as a whole which differs from the previous idea where the body alone is disconnected from our thoughts and without the influence of our other bodies. With this approach, you can actually cut down on time and wasted energy visiting numerous doctors who address ailments separately without seeing the bigger picture of how the mind, body, and spirit work together.

Choosing to understand and listen to your being, you are not only able to heal, you also can discover the root cause of why and how the illness developed in the first place. During this process, I discovered I created the osteopenia in my body because I felt a lack of support in my marriage, my finances, and my life in general. I was carrying a burden way too heavy to bear and my lower back and hip pain were a manifestation of those emotions physically. I healed Type 2 diabetes by simply acknowledging I was dealing with feelings of rejection and feeling I was "not enough" in my relationships. Forgiving myself and others for my perceived shortcomings released me of diabetes.

The physical ailments plaguing my body endlessly only indicated the emotional upsets I'd experienced and thus stored within my Emotional Body. This healing didn't occur until I was ready to take responsibility for what I was creating both from fear and from love. Healing our body and spirit is a cooperative effort. Our bodies heal when we're finally willing to address the emotional issues we've created and are now manifesting. Once this has been done, we're able to access the power within and begin creating a healthy, vibrant life again on our terms.

There's no judgment in holistic healing. Healing is simply a process of taking responsibility for your emotional, mental, physical and spiritual state, correcting what's wrong, what isn't working, and manifesting what's truly desired—better health. Fear, rejection, guilt, anger, blame, resentment—all these emotions are stored within our body if we don't release them as they occur. Failing to feel and listen to what your body is saying to you through your emotions means unfortunately allowing needless suffering to occur.

For instance, let's say you're sitting at the kitchen table eating cherries. Your mother walks into the kitchen and says your father has just died. In an effort to protect you from experiencing that deep loss ever again, you may acquire an allergy to cherries. The allergy is actually a coping mechanism developed by your body and mind to protect you from emotional pain. However, it's not the solution to recovering from a loss. The discovery of how to truly recover is available, and the answer to overcome any trauma exists within. You actually have the power to turn it around.

I'll use this example of developing an allergy to cherries. Let's say its five months since your father has passed and you finally sit down to eat another bowl of cherries only to find you have an immediate sick reaction to eating them. In this moment the average person says, "What the heck! Do I have an allergy to cherries?" What you can do is realize the allergy is created from a traumatic experience and ask your body to release the trauma associated with cherries. See, it's not about complication and a big elaborate process. It's about building love and trust within yourself, then consulting yourself to create the healing and changes you desire.

One question you can use to engage your being and have the allergy cleared is, "What does it feel like to find all the emotions and belief systems that created this allergy and allow it to be healed and freed from me?" Truly, in the matter of just a few minutes your body is healed of the allergy because you afforded your spirit the freedom to heal the block which the trauma created.

In regard to allergies, our bodies create them because of a perceived trauma which happened while we're engaged with that food, object, or animal in some way. However trauma is an extremely relative term. What could seem absolutely traumatic in one moment because of your emotional state may be laughable only days later. A child can walk down the sidewalk eating an ice cream cone, trips over his shoe, drops his ice cream and scrapes his knee. In that moment of "trauma" his body says, "I never want that to happen again." So it creates an allergy to the milk most people will unknowingly let rule them the rest of their life. Because of the disconnect within ourselves and between our four bodies, our Emotional Body doesn't realize it's okay to let go of the "trauma." It's already locked in and forgotten about, even when we consciously or mentally let it go days later.

The Physical Body continues paying the price for the Emotional Body's kneejerk reaction by keeping the allergy because the trauma is stored. Isn't that crazy? We create so much grief and struggle for ourselves because of the disconnection within us. Often we keep looking for answers outside ourselves because we don't trust ourselves enough to know the answers. Or, we don't believe we have the solutions and thus we get lost in the search for solutions somewhere "out there."

Give yourself permission to start listening to the unique rhythm of your body. We really don't want to be in pain, live with disease, or any ailments. The pain you may be experiencing is a last ditch attempt by your body to grab your attention physically so you can heal different emotional areas in your life where there may be disconnect, a break, frustration, or fear. Once you do the healing in the four bodies, the pain or disease will quickly leave your body. It's that simple.

In her iconic book, *Heal Your Body*, author Louise Hay writes:

> Both the good in our lives and the dis-ease are the results of our mental thought patterns which form our experiences. We all have many thought patterns that produce good, positive experiences, and these we enjoy. It's the negative thought patterns that produce uncomfortable, unrewarding experiences with which we are concerned. It's our desire to change our dis-ease in life into perfect health.
>
> We have learned that for every effect in our lives, there is a thought pattern that precedes and maintains it. Our consistent thinking patterns create our experiences. Therefore by changing our thinking patterns we can change our experiences.
>
> What a joy it was when I first discovered the words 'metaphysical causations.' This describes the power in the words and thoughts that create our experiences. This new awareness brought me understanding of the connection between thoughts and the different parts of the body and physical problems. I learned how I had unknowingly created dis-ease in myself and this made a great difference in my life. Now I could stop blaming life and other people for what was wrong in my life and my body.

Healing isn't dependent on your intellectual capacity, you don't need a high IQ to heal, but rather, healing occurs by restoring the energy flow throughout the body. It's available for everyone regardless of spiritual beliefs. Our Creator created you to be whole. It's your gift given from your Creator; you can experience this gift always.

Tool Four: Mapping Your Body

First we'll begin with a body-mapping exercise: Look with anticipation for the very first glimpse of information that comes to you and then listen intently.

Ask yourself, "What's my body telling me with this _____?"

For example, you might say, "What's my body telling me with this knee pain?" or, "What's my body telling me with this headache?"

You might get an answer that's a single word, or it could be a picture or a phrase. Trust the answer that comes to you. This answer is your intuition or Spiritual Body at work showing you your truth. The more you listen carefully, the more you can trust it. Therefore, your answers will flow to you with ease and little effort. If you're struggling to come up with an answer, research what physical responsibilities fall on the part of your body you're inquiring about in the charts provided previously. Once you've studied them, see how those responsibilities may resonate with an area of life in which you're currently experiencing emotional upset. For example your shoulders carry weight and bags, so is anything emotional like a weight holding you down?

Once you get a response ask, "What does my body want me to do about this _____?" Wait with anticipation for the answer to arrive and then trust the first bit of information that comes to you. It's there; trust the answer will come to you from within.

Many times your body just wants to release the emotions and beliefs being stored because they don't serve you and your highest good. Because of this, letting things heal is quite simple. You can do the process above, which I encourage as you begin tuning into yourself. It will help you develop your intuition and see cause and effect within yourself.

However, if you're ready to let things go, you can pose this question with any pain or discomfort that arises: "What does it feel like to find all emotions and belief systems that have created _____ and allow them to be healed and freed?" This question is so powerful, don't be surprised when your pain significantly decreases or completely goes away.

Ryan came to me with a severe problem in his right shoulder; his rotator cuff was completely destroyed for about three years. He couldn't lift his arm up over his head or even bring it level with his shoulders. He was definitely restricted with his movements and what he could do with his right arm.

I began working with him, talking to him about the emotions frequently stored in the shoulder. As I was describing the emotions that often accumulate there, he was nodding his head in agreement. The majority of the emotions I talked about applied to him. I asked him if he was up for me trying a few things to see if they would finally fix his shoulder.

His response, "I'm willing to give anything a try, but I'm not sure it will do much good because I just don't have a rotator cuff anymore."

I smiled at him and said, "That's alright. Let's see what your body can do."

In a mere fifteen minutes he went from extremely limited range of motion in his shoulder, to having 100 percent of his range of motion restored. All I did in those few minutes together was ask his body pertinent questions to heal the emotions and belief systems that created his injury in the first place. He left floored because he couldn't understand how it could work. But the proof was in the pudding; he had his shoulder back and was functioning again. He was amazed.

I have a mini coaching session and additional tools available at my website to help you develop this tool. You can access them at

http://www.joannaashley.com/embracing-your-truth/

and go to chapter 5 resources.

6
Nothing Is Impossible for You

Learn to control your thoughts and you have mastered your world.
—Lao Tzu

Sixty-five thousand thoughts pop up and flow through your mind every day. That's a lot of energy flowing through your body, emanating out to the world. Have you ever paid attention to the thoughts and feelings you entertain day by day, hour by hour, and moment by moment?

- Are they positive or negative thoughts and feelings?
- Do you find yourself thinking about yesterday or things that happened earlier today?
- Are they on a loop over and over again with little creativity?
- Or, do you think of fresh, new ideas and seek solutions?

Sixty-five thousand thoughts a day—all these thoughts coursing through your mind daily can create a great deal of mind clutter, but there's always a solution to help you calm down and focus. You can do something positive about all the things you feel and the thoughts you think. When you understand how to use your feelings and thoughts to make your life better, you will experience that nothing is impossible for you, especially when you use your imagination.

Our feelings are actually created from the Emotional Body but are felt in the Physical Body. In contrast, our thoughts are generated in the Mental Body as a result of what's stored in the Emotional Body as well. When you take a proactive approach to being conscious and self-aware of what you feel and think, you significantly reduce the power of your Emotional Body or the power that past experiences have to influence and alter your life. In this place of consciousness and self-awareness, you can truly begin stepping into the role of creating your life.

You're taking your existence off the autopilot flight plan generated in the Emotional Body. Now you can begin choosing what you want to experience and have in your life.

Your Creative Imagination is the Key to Life

There's immense power in your imagination and your ability to create. It's about you forming new ideas, concepts and realities within your mind, felt within your Physical Body. Interestingly, the word "imagination" comes from the Latin verb "imaginary" which means "to picture oneself." We use our imagination to manifest what wasn't previously available to our senses. At one time it was declared that flying was impossible, and running a four minute mile could never be accomplished. Yet in 1954 Roger Bannister finally ran the mile in four minutes. Since then over a thousand other runners have done so as well.

Your body responds to the power of your feelings and thoughts, and your feelings and thoughts create your reality. Before Rome was built, it was imagined. Before you started reading this book, you started imagining solutions to your problems. When you're able to use your imagination for positive creation, you're accessing creative energy that manifests a consciousness which transcends any obstacles or difficulties.

The Universe is made of Love Energy which is always moving and endlessly flowing. You're directly connected to the Universe and to Love Energy through your spirit. Because we exist in a dynamic universe full of energy, we use this to create. When you fall into the trap of using negativity including pessimism, fear, doubt, unforgiveness, and other similar emotions, you create blocks and obstacles that stop or restrict Love Energy from flowing.

Visualize a river flowing freely with a gentle, consistent force. Now gather twigs, logs, and mud and place them in the middle of the flowing river. What happens? The flowing current begins to slow, going around the obstacles as best as possible. Should enough twigs, logs, and mud build a dam, the water flow will stop completely. This is how fear and negativity can interrupt your life.

When this happens it's impossible to heal your body, find solutions to problems concerning money, relationships, health, and live with purpose to make your dreams your reality. Your formerly fun, creative imagination becomes drained and tired. When these stops are opened again, restored and healed to a positive place, we can once again manifest a powerful existence with triumph, joy, and peace. When we clear them, we open the abundant flow of Love Energy again.

It's not enough to be "a mindful person" because this alone won't create the change you seek in your life. To experience a life with purpose and passion, align your feelings and thoughts with your positive intention. That means you're in tune with your attitudinal state and your feelings and thoughts about the events you experience. Be aware of your feelings and the energy you're using because this creates your reality. Your intentions actually create your reality.

Creating the life you truly want means choosing to respond to the circumstances swirling around you rather than reacting to them. Responding to life means making careful decisions and choices that move you toward maintaining feelings and thoughts that resonate with your desired outcome. In contrast, when you react to life, you're simply responding in a kneejerk way, without focused feeling or thinking about the choices you have in the matter.

If you think about sickness a great deal, you'll manifest and experience sickness. If you're doubtful and full of concerns, real or imagined, you'll go up and down in life; happy one moment, sad the next. People spend years in therapy and never experience peace because they fail to connect their feelings and thoughts with the reality of their life. For ages now, many experts have come to show us the ways to strength, power, and vitality. All these experts unfailingly point to the power of our feelings and thoughts.

In a wonderful article written by mega-bestselling author, Dr. Wayne W. Dyer, "*Inspiration and Purpose,*" he discusses being inspired by great purpose. "*When you feel inspired, what appeared to be risky becomes a path you feel compelled to follow. The risks are gone because you are following your bliss, which is the truth within you.*"

No one can create your life; they have their own life to create. You create your life. People can tell you what to feel and think all day long. However, how do you know if they're right if you haven't sought out the truth yourself? Your feelings and thoughts are prime examples of what you truly think about yourself and how you see the world. The responsibility for your life and your experiences is in your hands. You have the opportunity to create it with style and flair. You can dare to live on the edge, live a peaceful existence or sit in the back seat of your life and let someone else drive the car. The choice is totally up to you. This is the beauty of life; it's yours for the making and for the taking.

Marci Shimoff, featured teacher in the documentary film *The Secret* and author of the New York Times bestseller, *Happy for No Reason*, says in her book:

> *Not surprisingly when your mind is swarming with automatic negative thoughts it has a profound psychological effect on you. Researchers at the National Institutes of Health, among others, have measured the flow of blood and activity patterns in the brain and have found that having negative thoughts stimulates the areas of the brain involved in depression and anxiety. On the other hand, positive thoughts have a calming, beneficial effect on the brain. Our negative thoughts are like poison in our system, and positive thoughts are like medicine...The good news is that to keep the thousands of negative thoughts we have each day from dragging us down, we don't have to try to get rid of each one of them. There's a simpler way. The secret is in accepting an astonishing fact: Your thoughts aren't always true.*
>
> *It sounds simple enough, but in fact, this revolutionary idea requires a major shift in our perspective. We're so accustomed to believing that our thoughts are true and automatically reacting to them, that we're hardly aware we're doing it.*

Shimoff's words remind us just because you think it doesn't mean it's infallibly true. Often our negative self comes up with, "What-ifs?" and "Woulda, coulda, shoulda" negative feelings and thoughts that don't help us grow as a person and experience a purposeful life. The positive feelings and thoughts you have are the ones to consider expanding upon and acting upon to help you heal, increase your confidence, be more adventurous, and create the vibrant, exciting life you want. It all starts with the power inherent in your positive feelings and thoughts.

Your Emotional Response Creates Your Outcome

According to the Heart Math Institute, heart-based emotional output is released at fifty thousand times the electromagnetic energy as emotions released from our brains. This means what you're creating in your life is done so from the core of your emotions. Spending a lot of time wallowing in fear, negativity, and lower level thoughts will only create lower level results. The sooner you're able to move past anger, fear, and depression or bypass these feelings altogether, the easier your life will run and the more you'll begin experiencing the healing, joy, and purposeful life you always wanted.

It's fascinating, there seems to be a real visceral connection between the heart and brain. They are constantly exchanging a two-way dialogue. It was once considered by scientists that the brain gave orders to the heart and then the heart obeyed. However studies show otherwise. As you begin experiencing more positive energy and mental clarity, your intuitive nature tends to increase, too. More than half of all doctor visits are stress-related.

The impact of our emotions on our health is profound. In a nutshell, where there is fear and negative vibes present, or restriction in the flow of Love Energy, you're bound to experience a poor mental state or poor health outcome. Numerous studies now show when you experience sincere and positive emotions, you will gradually have an increased immune system and forecast a better future because you honestly feel you can effectively solve problems and meet the day-to-day demands and challenges of your life.

In his classic book, *The Power of Positive Thinking* originally penned way back in 1952 by author Dr. Norman Vincent Peale, he writes:

> *My own heart specialist and good friend Dr. Louis F. Bishop says: 'It's not generally realized how many cardiovascular symptoms can be produced by tension and anxiety. Anxiety states are very common, and whereas it can be stated that a certain amount of anxiety is good for everybody because it spurs you to get things done,*

> *at the same time it can be very crippling. It may produce symptoms affecting almost any organ of the body.'*
>
> *'The heart itself reacts in various ways to anxiety. The rate may be remarkably increased; the rhythm may be affected; a stressful or anxious situation may produce a serious irregularity of the heart.'*
>
> *...But don't be alarmed. You've the power to overcome fear. It need not be allowed to harm you at all. The great fact is that you can, if you will, do something constructive about what you're afraid of. The ability to do this is one of the greatest results of positive thinking. Positive thinking presupposes a firm mind control. When you control your thoughts you'll be able to control your emotions, including fear and worry.*

Science knows so much more now than back in the 1950s when Peale wrote the book for which he's most remembered. Even back then doctors knew stress and negative thinking were powerful forces creating a physiological impact on not just our hearts but our entire bodies. In more recent years, scientific studies in prestigious medical research centers like Harvard Medical School and John Hopkins have further solidified the link between the state of our emotions and our health.

Everything is connected and it all begins with our feelings and thoughts. Those pesky things, if allowed to run freely, can and will make a big difference in your health and your level of success at living and experiencing the passionate life you desire.

While on the journey of healing my body of fibromyalgia and arthritis, I became pregnant for the first time which was exhilarating as we were struggling with infertility as well. Unfortunately, I lost our first set of twins due to a miscarriage. My depression was so deep I became temporarily suicidal. Although I was healing from fibromyalgia and arthritis, experiencing the loss of that precious life inside me caused me to spiral into a deep despair with feelings and thoughts like, "I'm checking out. I'm no good for anyone." Fortunately, the energy healer I was working with saw I'd sunk into an extremely low depression and urged me to get professional help.

I scheduled an appointment with a doctor and arrived at his office with my husband. The doctor asked me a lot of questions. In my many silent responses to his questions about contemplating taking my life and having a plan to do it, my husband for the first time learned I had serious thoughts of taking my own life. My doctor prescribed an antidepressant with a scheduled check-up date in the future.

After leaving the doctor's office, while sitting in our pickup truck, my husband turned to me and said, "Don't you know I love you?" Prior to this revelation from my husband, my emotions and belief systems at the time told me he couldn't possibly love me—disease, infertility, all of it. They told me he deserved better and I was holding him back, so checking out was the right thing to do. I learned just how wrong I was.

For those readers who have ever considered suicide, there's an invisible backpack many people seem to carry around. That backpack, sometimes called "emotional baggage" is filled chockfull of fears, resentments, regrets, blame, and torments too great to bear for many people.

The strength of our mind and possessing firm mind control, as Peale says, diminishes in vitality as we watch our life-force gradually leave our body when failures mound up and appear larger than life. If you've felt suicidal at one time, you know although you may often brush the thoughts aside, you may have a tendency to shrink into the shadows of death wanting so badly to escape the agony because you're uncertain how to get up and move on with your life. If you've had points in your life where you're gripped by death through despair, you may have believed you're unable to connect with the flowing energy of life to create change. I hope you'll be relieved to know there's a way out of the muck and mire.

The depths of suicide run deep in people unable to find the solutions to live happily with peace and understanding leading the way. There's no blame, shame, or guilt for those who have considered the world would be better without them. This is a personal journey for each of us and recovery is sweet when you finally move past those powerfully negative thoughts and accept your value is worth more than rubies or gold. One of the first steps to healing yourself is that of forgiveness and compassion.

> *Forgiveness does not change the past, but it does enlarge the future.*
> —Paul Boese

Forgiveness and compassion for yourself are essential elements to healing your life and your circumstances. Forgive yourself for:

- Not feeling adequate
- Not being a perfect son or daughter
- Hurting another person

When you do this you'll open the door to compassion and kindness for yourself. It's here you discover true connection to the Love Energy waiting in abundance for you. If you're currently struggling with depression or suicidal depression, please reach out to those around you. And if you can't bring yourself to do that please, listen to this special message I've prepared for you. Access it at:

http://www.joannaashley.com/depression-help-me/

It's easy to continue beating yourself up for having failed someone or because you can never get it right. It's easy, but it will leave you feeling miserable about yourself and your life. Honestly, beating yourself up only leads to more things happening which causes you to beat yourself up more. It's a vicious cycle. Over time you can become resentful, pitiful, and numb to living with emotional integrity.

When you choose to forgive yourself first, you can finally extend the same compassion to others and keep the peaceful energy flowing. Do this and you'll create a peaceful, sane environment where you can create and manifest a life of purposeful intentions and results.

There's no judgment in healing. There are no limits to how deep your compassion for yourself can go. Forgive it all. You're deserving of forgiveness and you're worthy of living a life filled with hope. It's incredibly easy to get trapped in the past and worry about the future, but today, right now in this moment, you've got the opportunity to create peace and positivity and release the anchor of un-forgiveness. It only requires the smallest change in your thoughts to begin soaring to new heights of compassion.

Every one of us is on a journey of self-discovery to learn lessons and grow to become the best we can be. Therefore, remembering this, you can exercise kindness and compassion toward yourself every day, every minute. We're all learning in one way or another, and the journey to learn love and appreciation for yourself is one, that if you choose it, you'll never regret. You'll not only feel better about yourself, your health will improve and your results and success will increase as well.

> *Healing takes courage, and we all have courage, even if we have to dig a little to find it.*
> —Tori Amos

Tool Five: Do the Impossible

Find a relaxing place in your mind for a few minutes. Create a picture in your mind of a relaxing scene. When you've got the picture in your mind of something that relaxes you and makes you feel peaceful and happy, ask yourself the following question:

"What does it feel like to find the emotions and belief systems that have helped me create my perspective about _____ and allow me to be healed and freed of them now?"

For example: "What does it feel like to find the emotions and belief systems that have helped me create my perspective about never really having what I want in life and allow me to be healed and freed of them now?" Or, "What does it feel like to discover the emotions and belief systems that have created my perspective that says I cannot do this and allow me to be healed and freed of them now?"

After asking the question, put your brain on vacation for a little while. Get your brain out of the way so your spirit can go to work bringing a resolution to the question. The reason the question is phrased this way is twofold.

One, to distract the brain so it's not trying to analyze and pick apart the possibilities based on logic. Your spirit's working on the question.

Second, it's also about combining a thorny problem and a possible solution into one question. To help you expound on these questions and take them even further go to chapter 6 resources:

http://www.joanna.ashley.com/embracing-your-truth/

Questions like these have helped so many people I've worked with to completely and totally transform their lives. Here is Eliza's story:

> When I was in high school I got pregnant just before I began my senior year. It was soon discovered that the father of the baby wanted nothing to do with either of us. I had to figure out how to do it on my own, since at this point I refused to see adoption as a possible option. Soon after finding out I was pregnant, I discovered I had genital warts. I was told they were incurable, and the condition would plague me the rest of my life; I was devastated by the blow.
>
> Towards the end of my second trimester I decided my daughter deserved more in life than a single mom who would be struggling to survive. So, I began considering adoption but I wasn't sure how I could ever be okay with that decision afterwards.
>
> I wrestled, deeply wanting to raise my daughter, but I also knew I'd never be able to give her the secure, happy life she deserved which broke my heart. However, it drove me to consider adoption even more, regardless of not believing I could possibly be okay afterwards, let alone ever be happy again.
>
> I soon found an amazing couple who had a daughter of their own but were now unable to conceive and ever have children of their own again. The mother befriended

me and loved me regardless of my situation. It was then I knew this was the family my daughter belonged in. When the day of my daughter's birth arrived, I got to love, hold, and cherish her for only a few hours. Then, tearfully I gave her over to her loving, new family. While giving her over to them I felt every piece of my heart shattering into a million pieces not knowing how I could ever be put back together again.

After placing my daughter with her adoptive family, I moved to Arizona to begin a new life. It was then JoAnna introduced me to many alternative means of healing my hurts. I was skeptical of what she offered at first until I began experiencing positive changes within myself, such as moments without sadness, something I never imagined possible since getting pregnant.

As I continued working with JoAnna, I began to hope again. It was then she told me she believed we could heal the genital warts. Once again, I was very skeptical but I decided it was worth a try. What did I have to lose?

I began using a series of oils, herbs, and energy healing techniques, facilitated by JoAnna, to release all the emotions and traumas attached to placing my daughter up for adoption and also those that had created the genital warts. Within three months all the warts were gone. Within six months I could no longer be diagnosed as having them. Four months after giving up my daughter for adoption I experienced the first sense of happiness and a deep, abiding hope my life would continue to get better. Also it was the first time I finally felt free to dream again and live a life filled with love and happiness; no longer did I carry the ominous, heartbreaking burden of placing my daughter up for adoption.

Almost four years later, my life is now better than I ever imagined. I'm married to the man of my dreams, and we have an amazing son whom we completely adore. I still get to see my birth daughter happy and loved every day with her family, through the beauty of the open adoption system. I *continue using the methods JoAnna taught me during the time we worked together.*

As a result I've freed myself of the limiting beliefs and emotions that used to have me in emotional and spiritual prison, living a life others told me I must live. Now I've embraced my own truth. I'm a co-Creator with God and I'm creating and living the life of my dreams.

7
Your Feelings and Thoughts Create Your Life. Use Them.

The experiences in your life are created by the feelings and thoughts you entertain over and over again as taught in the previous chapter. Whether you immediately see results or not doesn't stop or impede the outcome from manifesting for you. What you meditate, or focus on, day and night will come to fruition in one form or another. Consider a beautiful house with great curb appeal. The outside is well maintained with a lovely driveway, garage, and perfect landscaping. The trees are manicured and the grass is the right shade of green—it's lovely and inviting. The house is the envy of the neighborhood and the neighbors would love to check out the inside.

However, walk into the house and you'll find disorganization, clutter, and disgusting sights in every room. There's trash on the floor, pictures halfway hung, cobwebs in the corners, thick dust on all the furniture, stains on the countertops and floor, and roaches racing all over the kitchen countertops and table because food was left out overnight.

Now compare this scenario to the Emotional Body and its impact on what the Physical Body feels and what the Mental Body perceives. There are plenty of beautiful people in the world, yet their feelings and thoughts don't align with beauty or love at all. In fact, most people are stuck on some repeating negative thought or collection of thoughts that steal their joy, rob them of their peace, and absolutely wreak havoc in their lives. Regardless of how beautiful the house is on the outside, it's already started depreciating in value on the inside.

The same goes for us. Our feelings and thoughts are constantly creating what we and others experience in the physical realm. To overcome the creation of negative experiences, we must elevate our feelings and thoughts, think higher to obtain our higher purpose, and open ourselves up to the creation that comes from the flow of Love Energy so we can experience the good things we truly want in life.

Feelings and thoughts have the power to create. Here's an example of thoughts in action. In 2007, a well-known Silicon Valley company launched a computer game controlled by the power of your thoughts alone. These high-tech games can actually read a person's mood and determine the player's ability to fire a weapon or play ping pong. Is that amazing or what? A computer game totally controlled by the energy we create—namely our thoughts. As fascinating as this development may be, this isn't the first time we've had the ability to see our thoughts in action.

Our thoughts are the driver and the Creator of our life, our circumstances and everything that appears before us in our experience. Before there was a car, someone had an idea about a vehicle powered without the energy of horses. In fact the first cars were known as horseless carriages. Before there was Google, it was first a thought. What would it be like to be able to look things up online without having to know a specific web address or domain name. How many feelings and thoughts do you think you have in a day? How many ideas do you come up with? You're so miraculously powerful. You're more powerful and creative than you probably give yourself credit for. You have the power to create *anything* you set your mind to accomplish. Therefore, feel the positive feelings and think the positive thoughts that are lovely and pure; focus your feelings and thoughts on what you *really* want in your life.

Many books and spiritual teachers can now be found that profess the notion of your thoughts creating your reality. One of the most compelling to me is *Ask and It's Given* by Jerry and Esther Hicks channeling the teachings of Abraham. In the book it says:

> *You were born with an innate knowledge that you do create your reality. And, in fact, that knowledge is so basic within you that when someone attempts to thwart your own creation, you feel an immediate discord within yourself. You were born knowing that you are the Creator of your reality, and although that desire to do so pulsed within you in a powerful way, when you began to integrate into your society, you began to accept much of the same picture that others held of the way your life should unfold. But still, within you today lives the knowledge that you are the Creator of your own life experience, that absolute freedom exists as the basis of your true experience, and that ultimately the creation of your life experience is absolutely and only up to you.*
>
> *You have never enjoyed someone else telling you what to do. You have never enjoyed being dissuaded from your own powerful impulses. But over time, with enough pressure from those who surrounded you who seemed convinced that their practiced way was more valid than your way (and, therefore ultimately better), you gradually began to release your determination to guide your own life. You often found it easier just to adapt to their ideas of what was best for you rather than trying to figure it out for yourself. But in all this adapting to your society's attempts to make you fit in and in your own attempt to find less trouble, you unwittingly relinquished your most basic foundation—your total and absolute freedom to create.*

You Give Your Feelings and Thoughts Power

How much value do you place on your feelings and thoughts? Do you let any old feeling move through your body or allow thoughts to enter through your mind without first qualifying their validity? Or, do you shun any feeling or thought that comes up against who you are and what you want to create for your life?

You have the power to align your feelings and thoughts with purposeful intent and manifest the lifestyle you want, the friends you attract and keep, and how you choose to express yourself. Through the media, the music you listen to, and the environment you live in, you are bombarded with lots and lots of both positive, the flow of the Love Energy, and negative, the restriction of Love Energy by fear. You can be at cause and create your reality or you can subject yourself to the whim of others—this is your choice.

Allowing negative and fear-based feelings and thoughts to run rampant through your body and mind isn't icing a beautiful, white kitchen with sparkling bright, shiny floors and sunlight streaming through the windows as a gentle, warm breeze softly lifts the curtains. It's a rather peaceful scene because everything is clean and well kept, but something horrible just happened. The family Labrador retriever just ran in from the backyard and tracked in a trail of muddy tracks on the formerly shiny floor. Wow!

This little illustration is similar to how our feelings and thoughts work for us. We let them go in and out of our body and mind, but do we qualify them first? Are we paying careful attention to them? Self-defeating or fearful feelings and thoughts, and everything in between, should be measured carefully and discarded if they don't serve our higher purpose over time.

You may not have the next thought that creates a new-fangled, multi-million dollar gadget, but what you feel, think, and consider today will manifest in your tomorrows.

Change is a constant part of life. It's one guarantee we know we have. To advance and move beyond hurt, pain, and illness, we must be determined to dive in and reinvent how we think and do things. As boxer Muhammad Ali once said, "It is lack of faith that makes people afraid of meeting challenges, and I believed in myself." I'm sure you have important dreams and aspirations, and you've admired people who pursue life and their passion with enthusiasm. In all of this, they maintain a "failure is not an option" attitude. Are you honestly so different from them? Do you think the Universe would divvy up gifts and talents only to the few and chosen?

Certainly not. You have the same arsenal to fire, aim, and land a bull's eye at any negative feeling you feel or negative thought that enters your mind. Your feelings and thoughts are the only thing separating you from the life you truly want.

Negative feelings and thoughts from yourself or others will always step in trying to deter you from living your dreams. They will flood in and in a heartbeat say, "You can't really have that house," or, "You'll never make enough money," or, "Who'll ever take you seriously?"

Now that you finally know this, you can also gain control by understanding once and for all *how* to combat those little devils when they rise up. In a little book titled *The Four Spiritual Laws of Prosperity*, author Edwene Gaines explores simple ways to move away from what you don't want and move toward what you do want. Sometime we need extra "encouragement" to leave behind that which isn't working. She writes:

> *A young woman named Lisa called me because she hated the job she was in, yet she couldn't bring herself to leave it. She desperately needed money and did not think she could find another job. Feeling trapped and miserable, Lisa said she didn't know what to do. Knowing the power it has to change lives, I started her on the 21-day 'no complaining' challenge and gave her several affirmations.*
>
> *Much later, Lisa called to tell me she did the 21 days faithfully. On the morning of the 22nd day, when she went to work, her boss attacked her physically. Shocked and frightened, she grabbed her things and ran out. All morning, she drove around in her car, crying and shaking, trying to remember the affirmations I gave her. The only one she could remember was, 'I choose to live in trust.' Lisa kept repeating this and finally went into a diner for a cup of coffee.*

The person who had sat in the booth before her left a newspaper behind. There Lisa saw an ad for a job she thought she could do. She called and the woman said, 'Come right over, we're interviewing today.'

The job seemed perfect for Lisa; the location was beautiful, the offices were pleasant and the people were friendly. Later that afternoon her phone rang, it was the woman who interviewed her calling to offer her the job at double her previous pay. Lisa started the next day.

When you don't move voluntarily, the universe gives you a swift kick to get you going. Because Lisa couldn't find a way to leave a bad situation, the universe threw her out. You must be willing to give up what you don't want to get what you do want.

Your Feelings and Thoughts Are the Key to Life

Step by step I was gradually learning how to harness the power of my feelings and thoughts. Each struggle, every victory pointed to my feeling and thoughts. I was more carefully considering how I viewed my history to how I thought about the Universe. My life clearly shows big leaps forward, positive growth, and an ever increasing clarity about my personal truth and what it means to me. Your feelings and thoughts are the sum result of cause and effect. The more you're willing to do something about it and empower yourself, the more you live and operate in your divine strength and power.

The power of change happens most dramatically in those moments when you're willing to *feel the feelings* you need to make a significant change.

People say they can see what it is they desire. However, I check in further asking them, "Do you feel it?" Feelings are the doorway to creation because they're powerful energy. Often I've asked a client "What is it you'd like to have?"

They regularly reply with, "I don't know what it looks like."

The beauty of addressing your feelings is you don't have to know what it looks like. By first deciding what you want to feel, you open the doorway to begin seeing what it looks like. Feelings attract images and images create the vision.

One of my clients wanted to live in a different house. Her current home was falling apart and daily having new issues and problems. So I asked her, "What does your new dream home look like?" She was stumped. She had no idea. She just knew she wanted something different and better than her current house. Then I asked her, "What does your new home *feel* like when you walk inside?"

She started listing an array of feelings. "I want it to be warm, soft, and comfortable." As soon as she started talking about what she wanted it to feel like, she started getting visions of what it looked like because her Mental Body began producing images that resonated with those feelings. How cool is that? You can begin envisioning and creating your dreams by first deciding what you want to feel and then the imagining part just happens naturally.

Feelings are energy and if we attempt to avoid them, whether "good" or "bad," we stop the Love Energy from flowing through us. This eventually creates blockages. Have you ever said, "I feel stuck?" Chances are you were blocking some emotions from coming through so you could grow, change, and take your experience of life to the next level. Some people never allow themselves the full range of emotions to feel sad or angry. Other people I've met and helped never allow themselves to feel happy or joyful.

An important thing to remember is what you resist persists. If you're trying hard to avoid an emotion, you'll continue to, "Avoid, avoid, avoid," rather than experience the Love Energy flowing through you so you can prosper. By giving yourself full permission to experience each emotion, you start opening the door to making better choices and making better choices opens another door to experiencing greater opportunity.

It isn't always easy to "feel deeply" especially if you never had the support that encouraged feeling and expressing your emotions, so it will take practice to allow those feelings to gradually sift to the top, but I assure you, it will be okay. Remember, feelings are energy. At the flick of a switch, by changing your belief and your perspective, you can experience an entirely new feeling. Simply decide it and then choose it. When you're motivated to change and improve your life, only then will you take on the immense personal responsibility of owning your thoughts and feelings and the effects they create in your body and in your life. You can do it just as you can do all things because what you have needed for your journey has always been within you.

Tool Six: Use Your Feelings and Thoughts to Create

To illustrate this tool, I'll give you an example first.

Take something small you would like to have happen that isn't overwhelming. Maybe you'd like a small amount of unexpected money, say $50, for a date night out with your partner or spouse. Think to yourself, "Maybe we can do it. What would it feel like to have the money come to me?" Every time you think about having a date night with your partner or spouse, feel the money in your hand—fifty dollars. Two crisp twenties and a ten dollar bill you'll need for the evening. Ask yourself, "How would it feel to find fifty dollars lying on the sidewalk?" Embrace that feeling for a moment.

The ability to create comes from continuously feeling what it is you desire. So like in this example, you would engage yourself in a way that allows you to feel what you want to experience.

So here is the step-by-step.

1. Decide what you want. Whether it is a new relationship, job, home, etc.
2. Decide what you want it to feel like. (Peaceful, exciting, joyous, harmonious, calm, beautiful, exhilarating, loving, supportive, carrying, stimulating, etc.)
3. Next start asking yourself questions like "What does it feel like for _____ to feel _____?" This could look like "What does it feel like for my new relationship to feel loving, supportive, caring and fun?"
4. After you ask this question, put your brain on vacation and feel the feelings that come.
5. Now every time you think of that situation, ask yourself what it would feel like to feel the desired outcome.

The more you do this and allow yourself to feel, the more you focus the flow of creating Love Energy in your life and bring about your results more rapidly. You can use music, pictures, words, fabric, and anything else you like to help you first feel the experience you desire and second see the experience you desire. Before you know it you'll have created your desired outcome.

I have a mini coaching session and additional tools available at my website to help you develop this tool. You can access them at

http://www.joannaashley.com/embracing-your-truth/

and go to chapter 7 resources.

Here is an example of one of my clients applying these very tools and seeing huge results:

> Lane came to me with a great deal of hesitation. His appointment with me was kind of a last ditch effort. He and his wife had been married many few years and in that time he never held a job for long. Most jobs he got paid very low wages. As a result most of his married life was spent being dependent upon minimum wage and welfare to survive.
>
> He was tired of struggling but he also felt he was destined to a life of poor-paying jobs he was always fired from eventually. Nothing in him truly believed it was possible for him to have gainful employment, and you could see that clearly manifested in his life.
>
> When I started working with Lane, he was working a job he didn't like, making only ten dollars an hour. The prospects for getting a different job were dismal in his mind and he felt completely inadequate in his attempt to start a new career. I utilized an expanded version of the tools I've taught you thus far with Lane. At first, the effects of our efforts seemed minimal to both of us. However, as time progressed it was amazing to see the gradual transformation all our "slow" work created.
>
> It has been three years since I began working with Lane, and since then he went back to school, is becoming certified in a field he felt he would enjoy, and now has a very good job which he loves making $25 an hour. He isn't a millionaire and it wasn't a get rich quick scheme, but he's now honestly and confidently making more money than he ever has in his life. He feels a great deal of self-assurance and has even embraced his skills of problem solving and communication. This has also impacted his ability to connect in better ways with his wife and children.
>
> If you told Lane three years ago this is where he would be at this point, he certainly would have laughed in

your face. Today he understands his feelings and thoughts are the critical clues to the belief system he's using. As a result, those thoughts and emotions are creating his life every day. He's actively aware and continually changing any feelings, thoughts, and belief systems that arise out of harmony with building the life of his dreams. He has recognized his personal truth and is now driven to live it full out.

8
The Key to Change Is Shifting from Judgment to Compassion

If you want others to be happy, practice compassion. If you want to be happy, practice compassion.

–Dalai Lama

In the last several chapters I've covered your four bodies, your feelings and thoughts, and much more information. However this is where everything comes together as a whole. This is where your ability to affect a real and lasting change in your life and the world begins. It comes together with compassion. Compassion is a unique response to the human condition in our world because it transcends judgment and the factors that make us different such as language, race, color, creed, and gender.

Compassion within humanity can easily be observed during times of distress and trauma. People automatically unite to help each other overcome obstacles and build systems for safety and support within their community or across the planet. It's a unifying trait of mankind and something which undoubtedly transforms the difficulties of life we all feel at times into something more manageable, doable, and lovable.

With compassion, lives are healed and the broken rise up to stand again with dignity and hope as they reach out to help others. It's a steady flow of Love Energy, pulsating through the consciousness of man, and it's available any moment we need it and want it for healing. Compassion is available for you at all times without fail.

What's compassion? Essentially its empathy, kindness, and an understanding we as humans share in our suffering, barriers, and triumphs. It's a gift to others and a gift to ourselves. When we share and express genuine compassion for others, we're being a little gentler on ourselves. To be a compassionate person who wants the best for others is a conscious choice.

Practicing compassion daily becomes easier and is perfected through the power of our intentional thoughts and actions. This is the bridge from judgment to love and from despair to hope. It's measured by how well we serve each other in times of need or simply on a whim. Compassion also is a powerful indicator of how well we care for and love ourselves.

There are two important points I want to address regarding compassion and its significance. First is to reinforce how we extend it toward ourselves. The second is how we express compassion toward mankind around us.

Compassion throughout the world is synonymous with mercy, tenderness, and kindness. During the course of the history of mankind, we've heard many leaders discuss and emphasize the importance of expressing and feeling compassion toward our fellow man. There are plenty of charitable organizations existing today whose purpose is to help different segments of our society who suffer with specific challenges providing compassion, support, and dignity in times of need. Compassion is the cornerstone of healing yourself and achieving success in life. Why? I believe it's because we're all pretty much floating around in the same boat called the human experience. Many of us strive for ideals of perfection, but most of the time we miss the mark. We learn to accept that doing well is a good thing. Perfection is mostly unattainable and a way of withholding compassion from ourselves. As a saving grace, compassion removes all judgments, resentments and fears. It's vital to our own personal evolution and in the lives of those we connect with every day.

An excerpt from the book *Love, Compassion, and Tolerance* by Dalai Lama, editors Carlson and Shield reveal compassion is a necessity not a luxury. Compassion is caring about the suffering of others, not coming from a place of pity but from a sense of, "We're all in this together," and recognizing if the fates were turned around it could be the person offering compassion whose experiencing trauma or suffering. The book states:

> *Love, compassion, and tolerance are necessities, not luxuries. Without them, humanity cannot survive. If you have a particular faith or religion, that is good. But you can survive without it if you have love, compassion, and tolerance. The clear proof of a person's love of God is if that person genuinely shows love to fellow human beings.*
>
> *To have strong consideration for others' happiness and welfare, we must have a special altruistic attitude in which we take upon ourselves the burden of helping others. To generate such an unusual attitude, we must have great compassion—caring about the suffering of others and wanting to do something about it. To have such a strong force of compassion, we must have a strong sense of love that, upon observing sentient beings, wishes that they have happiness—finding a pleasantness in everyone and wishing happiness for everyone, just as a mother does for her sole sweet child. To have a sense of closeness and dearness for others, use as a model a person in this lifetime who was very kind to you. Then extend this sense of gratitude to all beings.*
>
> *Deep down we must have real affection for each other, a clear realization or recognition of our shared human status. At the same time, we must openly accept all ideologies and systems as a means of solving humanity's problems. One country, one nation, one ideology, one*

system is not sufficient. It's helpful to have a variety of different approaches on the basis of a deep feeling of the basic sameness of humanity. We can then make a joint effort to solve the problems of the whole of humankind.

Every major religion has similar ideas of love, the same goal of benefiting through spiritual practice, and the same effect of making its followers into better human beings. All religions teach moral precepts for perfecting the functions of mind, body, and speech. All teach us not to lie or steal or take others' lives and so on. The common goal of all moral precepts laid down by the great teachers of humanity is unselfishness. Those teachers wanted to lead their followers away from the paths of negative deeds caused by ignorance and to introduce them to paths of goodness. All religions can learn from one another; their ultimate goal is to produce better human beings who will be more tolerant, more compassionate, and less selfish.

In Southern Africa the Babemba tribe treats people who step out of line in a remarkable way. Instead of treating the person with judgment and punishment, the tribe treats the offender with love and appreciation.

If a member of the Babemba acts irresponsibly or unjustly, he or she is placed at the center of the village, alone. All work ceases. The entire tribe gathers in a large circle around the violator. Each person in the tribe, regardless of age, speaks to the accused, one at a time, recalling the good things the person in the center of the circle has done during his or her lifetime.

Every incident, every experience that can be recalled with detail and accuracy is recounted. All the individual's positive attributes, good deeds, strengths and kindnesses are recited carefully and at length. No one's permitted to fabricate, exaggerate, or be facetious about the accomplishments or positive aspects of the person. This tribal ceremony lasts several days and doesn't end until everyone's drained of every positive comment about the person in question.

At the end, the circle is broken. The person is symbolically and literally welcomed back into the tribe with joyful celebration. (Excerpted from *Contact, The First Four Minutes* by Leonard Zunin).

This cultural tradition speaks volumes about how the Babemba value human life. I'm moved by the idea that even though a person has committed an offense, they still express love and compassion toward him or her. So often, we have the opportunity to judge others for "offenses" committed against the community, but ultimately this doesn't help anyone.

Think of your own life when you've made mistakes, regardless of how big or small they may have been. In that moment realizing the mistake you made, or when you lashed out at others, did you feel good? I imagine it's safe to say you actually felt awful. Now being in a place of regret, shame, guilt, or whatever else you were experiencing, imagine someone stepping in, yelling, and chastising you for your mistakes and telling you how horrible and awful you were as a person.

Would you feel empowered and motivated, or would you believe it possible for you to change? I'd venture to say that you'd feel more defeated and awful and want to crawl in a hole.

Now let's consider this situation differently.

There you are wallowing in your shame, guilt, and regret and the person you wronged came to you and said, "I trust you're a good person and I know we all make mistakes. Please, don't be hard on yourself. I know you'll try to do better in the future. We all have 'human' moments. I forgive you and look forward to you forgiving yourself too," and then promptly gives you a sincere hug. What would that do for you in your ability to become a better person and not make the same mistakes in the future?

In the Broadway production of *Les Misérables*, there's a beautiful line, "To love another person is to see the face of God." In love or compassion, there's no judgment. There's only kindness, patience, and understanding. It's always about seeing the best in another regardless of the circumstances, the trauma, or the challenges.

Compassion towards another person has the power to heal because it's Love Energy and kindness flowing to that person which supports their own unique journey. True transformation doesn't occur through fear, judgment, anger, or hate. Instead transformation happens when love is extended with grace, granting importance, respect, and dignity to each other. The Golden Rule still applies in almost every spiritual tradition around the globe, "Treat others how you want to be treated."

In other words, how do you want other people to treat you? If you did something "bad" or made hurtful remarks, would you want people to stare back at you harshly? Would you want others to gossip about you behind your back or say insensitive things like, "He'll never change?" Certainly not. Knowing this, you have the opportunity to treat others with the same kindness and respect you would appreciate. This doesn't mean others will never cause harm or upset, but it does mean you're being true to yourself which will inspire others to follow suit.

When I was younger, I had a profound realization about myself with regard to compassion and my feelings about expressing concern for others. There was a homeless man named Mark in our town who my parents invited to live with us in our home. He was an older gentleman, but his presence grew on me.

Over the year of living with us, I came to consider him like a brother. One night while at a local park, a group of young boys my brothers and I went to school with beat Mark nearly to death and left him for dead in the park. He was found by local police and rushed to the hospital, only to die later from his injuries. People in the community were angry with this group of boys because they committed a deadly crime, murder, against someone else. At first I was furious, I sobbed, I was heartbroken. I felt deep loathing and anger towards these three boys.

Then it dawned on me, "What possibly happened in their lives to make them devalue this human life so much they would take it away?" Just asking myself this question completely shifted my perspective. I was able to move from a place of judgment and even hate towards them to a place of compassion and a yearning to want to understand what happened in their lives and what could be done to help them heal so they would make better choices in the future.

Compassion isn't necessarily based on logic.

The Old Testament verse "an eye for an eye" is antiquated and leaves everyone in a place of fear, discomfort, or even worse, hate. To have and express compassion doesn't mean the guilty party should not have to face the legal consequences of their actions if one commits a crime. Rather, compassion acknowledges the value of everyone, even the guilty.

Compassion is an active, viable force of energy used to show you care for others who may be less fortunate. When you operate from a position of love rather than fear, you inspire and create the impossible. By advocating the importance of others, you help rebuild their self-esteem again. Compassion demonstrates they can have a life without fear or guilt. It's a gift you can give others, and more importantly, you create a positive, supportive environment around others and yourself.

Compassion is the root of positive change. I know this all too well. When the memories of sexual abuse returned to me like a flood of high definition videos, there were many people around me who stated that I would never be the same again. I had the right to be angry with my abusers, and they said I would struggle to overcome the anger and effects of the abuse for the rest of my life. I could have easily allowed the opinions of these "supportive people" to influence how I felt about myself and those who harmed me. Instead I decided to choose compassion. Not only did I heal from this atrocity, but I chose to hold to the viewpoint that the people who abused me could use understanding and compassion instead of judgment for their transgressions.

I decided I would not hold them in contempt and anger in the box of judgment but in its place forgiveness. Because if I placed them in a box of resentment, anger, or apathy, I'd be the one who would pay the mental and physical price the rest of my life. Additionally, nothing would be done to allow them to heal themselves, either.

I know this suggestion can be rather controversial to some people, and I understand a person wanting to inflict suffering on another who brought suffering to an innocent child. But I firmly believe doing the best you can to heal from trauma caused by another means first extending compassion and love to ourselves and then to others, for compassion doesn't discriminate.

When you refuse to forgive someone for their wrongdoing, you become stuck in a trap of your own making. The moment you choose to hold on to grievances, bitterness or grudges, you allow an emotional poison to affect your physical and spiritual health negatively. This creates a victim attitude and when you see yourself as a victim, you have no control. Empowerment is impossible. A victim mindset also creates a chain of "unforgivable moments" some people use to:

- Keep others away
- Relive painful moments to get sympathy from others
- Stop experiencing joy in life due to feeling unworthy
- Feel shame and humiliation because they believe they deserve it

More often than not, our society advocates reacting with judgment and ridicule when a wrong is committed—it's expected. After all, most of us grow up with expectations of what's right and what's wrong. When you were a young child, you were expected to sit behind a desk at school, be attentive, and above all else behave as the teacher insists. Your parents probably placed certain expectations upon you like get good grades, obey your elders, clean up after yourself, and be good at sports. When you finally became an adult you were expected to live in a box on this block and do this job because it's *expected*.

Compassion erases all expectations from us and invites us to *come as we are*. There's true freedom when we actively use compassion. The pain of loss or failure disappears and hope is restored again for the possibility of a brighter tomorrow.

Here is a quick piece of trivia: Did you know a whopping 80 percent of illness is created by unresolved resentment? Resentment and blame are often the leftovers that fester after refusing to forgive. Not only is compassion a creative, powerful force, but the lack of it can actually cause illness. I think it's time to get healthy by forgiving and expressing compassion.

Love Repairs the Unrepairable

Love, compassion, and forgiveness always start with you. Without these core elements, life can become tough and burdensome. These three characteristics are the building blocks for developing true inner strength and perseverance. There's a thought some people believe—if you use compassion toward another, you'll be taken advantage of, or you'll become a doormat for others. However, this is faulty reasoning.

Actually, the opposite is true. When you sincerely activate love and compassion in your life, you'll attract more love, inspiration, hope, tolerance, justice, kindness, and forgiveness from others should you miss the mark or suffer a traumatic experience. The grace and kindness you extend to others will return to you. The pain you may experience for extending kindness will be temporary because grace will abound, setting you and others free over the course of time.

The power of love can totally fix the things we think are irreparable forever. You have the power to change your mind instantly. All you have to do is make a different decision about things. You may not be able to change another person's decisions about forgiveness and compassion; however, you can choose to treat each individual you come across with love and hope which ultimately can inspire their greatness.

It's only our belief system that limits our ability to live a compassionate life. That's all. But when you halt the need for rigidity, boxes, and expectations that trap people, they will vanish. This is true freedom and freedom is a choice we get to make.

Compassion Is for You, Too

I've discussed extending compassion towards others. It's a good thing because it creates freedom and release from anger and resentment. But ultimately freedom starts with you. That means you must also extend kindness and compassion towards *yourself*. We rarely hear about this and it seems like such a foreign idea. When you progressively evolve, you learn the gentle art of being nice to yourself every day. No matter what happens, you'll inevitably experience a powerful and *unshakable* inner peace, sincerely extending it to others. We often place expectations on ourselves regarding how we should be or what we should do as a result of our upbringing. You may buy into the latest version of what Hollywood or the media says should be expected and from those you associate with including your friends, family, and work associates.

A lack of compassion for you increasingly manifests due to negative self-judgment about your missteps, failures, or transgressions. We can say things to ourselves that cut us down to the core and invalidate our personal worth. You may say things to yourself like:

- I'm not good enough
- I'm so stupid
- I'll never get it right
- No one will love me
- I'm worthless

Need I say more? These all stem from an unrealistic or unattainable expectation you've placed on yourself. Like a heavy burden you may use statements like these when you seemingly fall short of your goals and beliefs. This is a profoundly negative judgment against who you really are, and it's the extreme opposite of compassion and love for yourself.

Remember, you're human and although you may strive for perfection at times, you probably won't always make the mark. Sorry to say, but it's true. Judgment is a negative energy force, and when used, it causes blockages and stops you from learning about the beliefs that truly matter to you. Therefore, show kindness to yourself by being supportive and encouraging of yourself.

Self-judgment and ridicule will suck you into an emotional black hole with no good or supportive purpose in your life. A little extra kindness goes a long way. Also, showing self-compassion means you're attentive to what you need and want for yourself. If you're in pain, suffering, or in need of tender loving care, give it to yourself generously rather than waiting for someone else to shower it on you.

It's okay to take care of your needs, too. You're just as valuable as the next person. Showing compassion towards yourself is a natural step towards winning in life and creating your own happiness. You're building a safe environment for yourself which is inviting and caring, and others will experience this energy from you, too.

Compassion is a powerful tool. It eradicates judgment, shame, doubt, fear, guilt, loneliness, and heals the body, mind, and spirit. It builds courage, strength, independence, harmony, creativity, and connects us to each other through support and understanding. Exercising compassion is a choice that takes steady practice. When used daily for yourself, you'll remove the need to judge yourself or another negatively.

You'll open your mind to be gentle when transgressions occur, and, rather than hold onto unforgiveness, you'll grant yourself and others importance, dignity, and love. This next tool will open the floodgates to a life filled with compassion joy and peace. Use it and have fun.

Tool Seven: A Life of Compassion

There are three important questions for you in this tool. After asking each one of the three questions, put your brain on vacation a little while before moving forward to the next question. Get your brain out of the way so your spirit can go to work bringing a positive resolution to the question. The reason the question is phrased the way you see it below is twofold. First is to distract the brain so it's not trying to analyze and pick apart the possibilities based on logic. Secondly, it's about combining a problem and a solution into one question.

In this tool there are three questions which gently move you from the place of impossibility to a place of knowing how to achieve what you desire.

1. "Disregarding my bias and opinion, what does it feel like to have God's truth and perspective on _____?"
2. "Disregarding my bias and opinion, what does it feel like to believe in the possibility _____?"
3. "What does it feel like to find all emotions and belief systems that are _____?"

Now let's apply these three questions. Let's say you're trying to forgive someone for committing an atrocious act against you. However, every time you try you're filled with more and more anger. The hurt runs so deeply you just cannot see how it is possible for you to overcome the hurt, violation, and devastation. This is how these questions look:

- "Disregarding my bias and opinion, what does it feel like to have God's truth and perspective on whether I can truly overcome this and be healed of this abuse as if it never happened?" Remember you're not thinking about an answer here, rather you're observing how you feel. Calm = Yes and Anxious = No. Most the time you'll get a calming feeling that whatever you're inquiring about is a possibility.

- Next you'll ask, "Disregarding my bias and opinion, what does it feel like to believe in the possibility of truly overcoming this abuse and being healed as if it never happened?"
- "What does it feel like to find all emotions and belief systems stopping me from healing from this abuse and allowing them to be healed and freed from me?"

While this may seem overly simplistic, these tools have proven powerful far beyond anything else I've ever implemented. I'd love to help you personally apply them in more ways, so I've created additional tools you can access at:

http://www.joannaashley.com/embracing-your-truth/

9
The Answers to all Your Questions Exist Within

According to an old Hindu legend, there was a time when all human beings were gods, but they abused their divinity. So, Brahma, the chief God, decided to take divinity away from them and hide it somewhere they could never find it.

Brahma called a council of gods to help him decide where to hide the divinity. "Let's bury it deep in the earth," said the gods.

But Brahma answered, "Humans will dig into the earth and find it."

Some gods suggested, "Let's sink it in the deepest ocean."

But Brahma said, "No, humans will learn to dive into the ocean and find it."

Then some gods suggested, "Let's take it to the top of the highest mountain and hide it there."

Brahma said, "We don't know where to hide it because it seems that there's no place on earth or ocean that human beings will not eventually reach." Brahma thought for a long time and said, "We will hide their divinity deep in the center of their own being. Humans will search for it here and there but they won't look for the divinity inside their true *selves." All the gods agreed this was the perfect hiding place, and the deed was done. Since then, humans have been going up and down the earth digging, diving, climbing, exploring and searching for something which already lies in themselves.*

Since the beginning of man's existence, we've been on a seemingly endless quest to discover who we are, why we're here, and what we're truly capable of achieving. Man's evolution throughout the centuries can be tracked in the course of history—we see it through the myriad of changes in our laws, religion, medical breakthroughs, and the push to connect with others and the earth. The effort to be greater and better than before is easily seen every New Year's Eve as we set resolutions and goals for the upcoming year like spending more quality time with family, losing weight, and traveling more. We have bucket lists, we take classes to improve our minds, read self-help books, and much more. We're always on a journey to improve, coming up with better and faster ways to achieve this or that. We're rather remarkable.

However, there's a last frontier traveled by few. That is the journey within to self-discovery and growth. The discovery of who we are isn't easily found. If it were, more people would be happier and more prosperous. Looking within only happens when you surrender to the idea that we all need help in one way or another. If this describes you, more than likely you have tried other avenues to know yourself and grow from the inside out. Look within—you must search past the illusion of the physical realm and tap into the current flow of our energy. This isn't to say the physical realm isn't real, but it doesn't exist without our intentional thought applied to it.

Perception is reality, so what you perceive in your unique vision is how you see the world around you. Life is full of complexities, and although we've created many religions to solve its riddles, there's only one solution. Listen to your inner voice. Go within to manifest what you need to thrive and achieve what matters to you.

What if I were to ask you, "Who are you? What's your name?" Would you say you are your body? Or, would you say instead, "I am me?" While these answers are partially true and if you haven't guessed yet, you are a spiritual being living here on earth having a human experience capable of creating miracles. Although you're using your body to sense the physical realm, you can be at cause and create a wonderful life full of rich understanding and wisdom.

Divinity is within us all. When I refer to divinity, I'm not stating you're usurping the power of God. Rather, I'm suggesting you are sacred and created in the image of God, and your body is a temple.

Whether you're a Christian, Buddhist, Muslim, Jewish, Hindu or none of these—you have the power to know, experience, and understand how to create, heal, and excel for yourself in this life. You're filled with unlimited potential and an ability to know anything you desire. No one can define your limits but you. When you accept and embrace this amazing gift from the Universe, you'll discover the answers you need for your life when you need them.

The idea that we have the answers within can be a foreign thought for many people—even a scary one. This is because most of us were taught to ask someone else for advice and guidance. We live in a society that doesn't consider our personal observation as a source of authority but places group agreement and authority above all else. We see this in government, organized religion, academics, the media, and other institutions we deal with on a daily basis. We're expected to conform to these "authorities" and "experts" and look to them to find our personal truth. The real matter at hand is *you* and how *you* see, feel, and think the about the world around you.

You can arrive at conclusions which foster wholeness, peace, healing, and joy on your own accord which may or may not agree with others.

Let me share with you a modern day story about a slum in Paraguay that's transformed trash into music, courage, and confidence and has transcended the norm in slum communities.

One day, a worker was raking through the trash heap at a landfill and found a shell of a violin.

This was the inspiration for creating musical instruments like violins and cellos from trash so children could learn to play music and focus on something positive. He never imagined this would be his path before, but he saw the opportunity to create something extraordinary.

In Paraguay, a violin costs more than a house, so the chances of a child from the slums owning and playing a musical instrument are slim. But one man, Favio Chavez the music teacher, with the help of Cola a local garbage picker and Luthier, started on a mission to transform trash into music so every child could have an instrument. He could have easily flowed with the attitude the community was too poor and some students would have to go without. He could've sought the "counsel" of others for their agreement and approval first. Instead he asked how he could use some of the trash to create instruments of beauty. Because of his willingness to see a solution regardless of how big the problem appeared, he not only created instruments, he transformed the lives of his students forever.

Within each of us is the ability to think outside the box and create a beautiful life by finding solutions to problems, not only for ourselves, but for those we interact with every day.

Change Your Beliefs and Change Your Emotional Response

Have you ever heard the expression, "Time heals all wounds?" If that were true, people would not be traumatized by the loss of loved ones twenty years later or feel spiteful over injustices committed many years ago. Many wouldn't live a bitter life if time healed all broken hearts. What I discovered instead was that time doesn't necessarily heal, but a conscious decision to heal does every time. The first two miscarriages I had were devastating and resulted in severe suicidal depression, anxiety, fear, and a completely crushed heart. Many tried to console me while others told me this was "normal."

Gratefully, my husband and I were blessed with our daughter after the first two miscarriages. Then I had a chance to apply what I learned about making a conscious decision to heal. My husband and I decided to try for a second child. This attempt resulted in four more miscarriages. However, I wasn't the broken, crushed woman I was after the first two because I realized I got to choose how I was going to be on the other side of the experience.

This isn't to say I wasn't angry, or I didn't cry, or I just went on as if life was all hunky-dory. However, I'm saying the miscarriages didn't destroy me. I channeled my hurt and instead focused on all the blessings in my life. I made a *choice* to allow myself to heal. When I figured this out, I knew the pain I felt at losing many babies through several miscarriages wasn't an issue of, "time mending my broken heart." But instead I came to see it was about a belief, and a belief can be changed instantaneously.

Once I changed my belief about "how" I was supposed to deal with these losses and instead embraced the truth my Spiritual Body, or intuition, was sending to me, I quickly overcame what once were soul crushing, suicide-inducing losses. We can adopt new beliefs and choose how we feel about an idea or a person or anything at any given time.

Belief is at the core of everything we say or do. We're motivated by our thoughts. When you change your beliefs, you change your emotional response to life and the circumstances around you. The ball is in your court and the ability to rise above the clattering noise of fear, anger, apathy or depression, relies on you. Your ability to understand your core beliefs and how they originated and then challenge the beliefs that no longer serve wholeness, peace, wealth, healing, joy, and abundance in all things can change your outcomes in a minute.

Friedemann Schaub, author of the ground-breaking book, *The Fear and Anxiety Solution*, suggests when we embark upon an inner journey, it's possible to quickly heal from the fear and anxiety holding you back from what you want. He writes:

The point where fear and anxiety start to interfere with our abilities to function in our lives certainly varies from person to person; however, there are clear indications when these emotions are becoming serious challenges and need to be addressed.

Some of these are:

- *Frequently feeling overwhelmed and worried*
- *Obsessive thinking, overanalyzing, and ruminating about the worst-case scenario*
- *Over planning and trying to control others and/or outside circumstances*
- *Growing difficulties with work and relationships due to insecurity, doubt, and self-sabotaging behavior*
- *Feeling paralyzed and stuck because of an inability to make decisions or move forward*

- *Seeking distraction and instant gratification in addictive behaviors such as gambling, eating, sex, or work*
- *Obsessive-compulsive behavior*
- *Self-medication with alcohol, nicotine, or other drugs*
- *Physical symptoms such as insomnia, high blood pressure, irregular heartbeat, chronic pain, and weight fluctuation*

Fear Is a Dream Snatcher

Here is an example—a first year financial planner is working hard to ramp up his career. To get clients to help increase his paycheck, he must set appointments and talk with people about money and their investments.

However, he feels fearful talking to people about these things because he's scared of rejection. The obstacle he faces is talking to people, and the emotional response is fear because he doesn't want to fail. His fear is based upon the belief he isn't enough. He believes he doesn't possess great communication skills, he isn't smart enough, or he doesn't know his products well enough.

He has a choice. He can choose to opt out of his career and find something "less challenging." Or, he can recognize his fears and choose to heal the underlying negative beliefs he has about himself.

Unfortunately most people will jump ship and try to find another less challenging position rather than look within and change their negative beliefs about themselves. But you've read this far, and that's a strong indication you're willing to look within and change what no longer serves you so you get the result you want for healing, for better relationships, for success, and more.

On my journey, I realized I couldn't stop fear from showing up, but I could learn how to refuse to let fear control me when it appeared. Fear is an ugly thing—it's a dream killer, a happiness snatcher and an anti-Creator. Fear, when used as an operating tool in your life can only choke the energy and excitement out of your hopes and dreams. Let fear run rampant and it will only consume you, leaving you high and dry. Fear leads to procrastination, a lack of creativity, and a sense the environment you live and operate in is dangerous.

It's the one thing preventing us from connecting with ourselves, our neighbors, family and friends. Fear attempts to "predict" the future by telling you about all the bad things that *could possibly* happen.

Seth Godin said it well, *Anxiety is nothing but repeatedly re-experiencing failure in advance. What a waste.*

The Universe Is Waiting for You

The best solution for overcoming fear is to stop it dead in its tracks and listen to your inner voice. Take your power back by creating your future with love. The things that are lovely, pure, righteous, joyful, funny, and inspiring create hope and inspire greatness in you. They unleash the abundant flow of Love Energy to create all things. These are the things your inner voice will promote and share.

This is what you need to find within. Even if it's only a tiny whisper within you, focus upon it and encourage it to grow. Our Creator and the Universe is working with you, not against you. It's listening to your every whim. That's why persisting in your own discovery for the truth and being determined to stay the course is important. The moment you begin your journey, the Universe will conspire to meet you and reveal the mysteries hidden within you so you can use them for your good.

In *Conversations with God*, author Neale Donald Walsch writes, *You are goodness and mercy and compassion and understanding. You are peace and joy and light. You are forgiveness and patience, strength and courage, a helper in time of need, a comforter in time of sorrow, a healer in time of injury, a teacher in times of confusion. You are the deepest wisdom and the highest truth; the greatest peace and the greatest love. You are these things. And in moments of your life you have known yourself as these things. Choose now to know yourself as these things always.*

Your feelings vibrate to the Universe attracting more joy, love, hope, or they will attract more fear, pain or anxiety. The origin of your feelings starts with a belief which creates a thought. Since you are a creative force, you'll manifest what you place your attention upon. When you turn to others for answers without trusting yourself, you betray yourself because you're not listening or looking at how you truly feel.

If you take the time to listen to the Spiritual Body you possess, you'll find your own compassion, trust and brilliance. You can build the confidence you need to stand on your own and live a life designed by your thoughts and feelings of how the universe should be according to your beliefs.

The Dalai Lama once said, "Don't look to others for what is right—look to yourself and do it."

There must be a point in your life where you finally say, "Enough is enough! I'm ready to stop the negativity and pursue happiness and wholeness."

Love Energy Flows through You

Love Energy will arrive for you when you become open and ready to receive. When you surrender yourself to the idea you can be whole and healed, your world will blossom and open for you. Love Energy is in everything that exists around us. It's a current flowing through you and me and there's no shortage of its availability. I learned to open myself up to this truth, and once I did, I was suddenly capable of solving my own problems and learning new ways of helping others. All negative emotions restrict or stop this Love Energy from flowing immediately. This happens when you feel low, worthless, and unable to do anything right for yourself or others.

These feelings are only an illusion because the moment you step past the veil of fear, you'll suddenly be able to open the doors to opportunity and experience the power of healing, wealth, and certainty.

You have an innate ability to create, dream up and manifest what you need and want for today and for the future. This means you have the power to bring forth things that didn't exist before. You might be surprised to read this, but you're actually the embodiment of Love Energy. You have the divine power to express what's needed for you, aligned specifically to your wants and needs.

The empires of the future are the empires of the mind.
—Winston Churchill

Give Yourself Permission to Be Truthful

Truth is completely dependent upon each individual and is, therefore, unique to each person—including you. When you decide to acknowledge the truth and embrace what that means for you, you'll position yourself in a place to create the life you want and rid yourself of unnecessary fear.

There certainly are times when I still feel fearful, but I remain conscious and mindful and decide how much power I'm willing to give to fear in my life. Once I decided to fully accept and express my truth, my family and friends entered a place of respect for my distinctive point of view. They can clearly see and have now experienced how I'm helping others through embracing my truth. They have also seen how it has helped me heal from all the ailments plaguing me.

Living your truth and owning how you feel create a straight road to peace within. There's no uncertainty or seeking in the sense of one who says, "I'm lost, please save me." Rather it's a joy of discovery and complete vulnerability because you get to "come as you are" and show up with no pretense. Without show or force, your communication gradually changes.

Those you speak with intrinsically know you're the real deal. Those people are willing to forge ahead and explore the depths of who they are and what they need to create a space within for their voice. They discover a space to honor their feelings and have the courage to allow others to do the same.

For those who believe they've healed and have found "completeness," they've made peace and finally accepted the good, the bad, and the ugly of others and themselves. They now grant importance to everything.

In my wildest dreams, I would have never considered writing a book to you. I also never predicted my future including the ability to develop a successful healing process that would help instantaneously change the mindset and beliefs of people struggling or in pain. I've received confirmation after confirmation that my GABE technique which I've been teaching you throughout this book is astonishing when it comes to helping others. It's easy to use, solid and reliable.

I once worked with a woman who sprained her ankle. I posed a question to her and as she answered, she suddenly gasped, "There's no pain in my ankle!" She got up from her chair, walked around, jumped up and down and just that fast, she was healed.

Can you believe it? By changing her belief about the thoughts she had within, she was healed.

Another woman came to me with a lot of negative, limiting beliefs about her life and the world around her. She suffered from insomnia. She believed she didn't have a choice about not being able to sleep, and it was necessary for her to "trudge" through life and suffer. I asked her a series of probing questions, but the main question I posed to her was, "What does it feel like to believe in the possibility that doesn't have to be this way?" This simple question cured her insomnia.

For the first time in ten years she slept well, and she continues to sleep through the night to this day. I continue working with her periodically to release her limiting beliefs, but you wouldn't know she was the same woman. She understands her true value and doesn't nickel and dime her fees for her services. Additionally, her personal connection to her Christian faith has transformed.

This truly inspired me because she believed in order for God to answer her prayers she had to grovel at his feet for attention and favor. She was so frightened of God before, but after working with her, she's discovered God is her best friend and He wants her to co-create the best things she can possibly have in life. Now, looking back at her thought patterns and beliefs, she laughs because she can see how limiting and irrational those beliefs were.

She's learning to accept responsibility for her outcomes in life and rely on her ability to achieve success financially and spiritually. This is the point of going within; it's to live a purpose easily seen by others and experience the full power of our creative abilities.

Living life by design requires a paradigm shift. Intentional living is about knowing you have the ability to heal, experience joy, and grow spiritually on your terms. This type of lifestyle no longer seeks the approval of others.

When you decide you can evaluate the truth for yourself, you'll no longer sit quietly behind a desk hoping to be noticed or ask for permission to speak. You'll gain the courage to authentically share your experiences with those who want to listen. You'll gain clarity about the road ahead before actively participating in manifesting your desires. Your voice will resonate with others on the same journey of living in truth.

The Truth within Will Guide You

We're shown in our culture that group agreement is necessary for survival through the media and the praise of Hollywood actors, actresses, teen idols, and more. The inner self is so often neglected and silenced by the noise of people telling us how to think, what to feel, and who to obey.

Granted, this is highly generalized and is not necessarily true for every person, but my point is we're not taught to trust our own voices first and foremost. Looking deep within to find the truth by asking simple questions will open the door to a new perspective. A higher truth will evolve into something beautiful and sustainable for you. Listening quietly and carefully to your inner voice cultivates greater strength and confidence. This is living a life from within yourself to influence your environment and others on your own terms.

In the book *Soul Love* by Sanaya Roman, the author explores easy, fast ways to connect with the energy of your soul and how it can aid in your transformation. She encourages you to take a wonderful adventure meeting your soul and learning to love yourself and others unconditionally as your soul does.

By now you know the more you vibrate and focus on Love Energy, the more fear falls away. Here's the vital role your soul plays in becoming more mindful, more loving and able to heal and manifest what you want. Roman writes:

> *Your soul does not judge you, you judge yourself. Decide you will put the past behind you, particularly those times you do not feel good about how you acted, what you did, what you said, or who you were. Be willing to forgive yourself instantly for anything that you do...*
>
> *Your soul's love is available to you all the time. Whenever you feel afraid, let your soul come into your heart and radiate its love to that fear. Whenever you feel helpless, vulnerable, or trapped, bring your soul into your heart and let its warm rays dissolve those feelings and help you find answers. Your soul is always sending you its soothing rays of reassurance, telling you that everything will be all right, that the universe is your friend, and there is always an answer to any problem.*
>
> *If you are feeling sorry for yourself, let your soul heal your feelings of self-pity so you can know the strength that is within you to create a life that brings you joy. Let your soul's compassion for others flow into your heart, recognizing the suffering of all human beings. As you experience an ever-increasing compassion and love for all life, you will find it harder to feel sorry for yourself. You will experience instead your soul's love for all life and its focus on loving others.*
>
> *If you feel unloved or unappreciated, feel the love and appreciation your SOUL has for you. Feel your soul's love come to you through the images it will send you of all the good things you have done, all the people who DO love you, and all the things that ARE working in your life. As you acknowledge all that is good and right about you and your life, you are experiencing your soul's love for you, for your soul lives in a state of gratitude and appreciation.*

Layers of fear and feelings of separateness can be released as you open your heart to your soul's love. Your heart center can become like a sun, radiantly transmitting the energies of love, compassion, forgiveness, healing, and acceptance to others, to you, your sub-personalities, and to the cells in your body.

As your soul enters into and stimulates your heart center, there will be a corresponding shift in the way you feel, think, and view your life. When your soul touches your heart, your focus of attention changes. You become more aware of love in all its forms. You choose those actions, words, and activities that are joyful and loving to you and to others. Old criteria, such as what brings you the most money, makes you feel secure, or gives you power will fall away. What becomes more important to you is finding work you love, following your heart, and trusting in the abundance and goodness of the universe.

With an open heart, you'll perceive people differently. You'll find their soul, and be more aware of their potential.

Having more tools to use to help you embrace what works and release what doesn't work is always a good thing. Looking to your soul is looking to the deepest places within.

What you're looking for is already inside. You are the total package—healed, delivered, set free, prosperous, intelligent, beautiful, and much more. Know that getting feedback from others and hearing their observations is valuable to you, but understand your decisions are valid and important. Trust your truth. Listen to your inner voice and not the inner critic drilled into your head by your mother, father, or school teachers. This will foster true wisdom, inspiration, and magnificence in you.

If you're not in tune with your intuition and you cannot tell your inner voice from the authority figures in your life, here are some examples of how to begin:

- Your inner voice is that little child tapping you on the shoulder. It's a gentle, non-invasive nudge letting you know, "Something is here."
Your authentic inner voice is always respectful of you. Intuition has manners that never invoke fear or anger but a calmness that brings a fresh perspective, new ideas, and greater ways to manifest what you want.
- Your inner voice is found when you take time to inquire and ask for input. Without force, your voice is most likely found waiting quietly within for your acknowledgment.

Listening to yourself is like art in motion. Your divine nature arrived here on earth, ready to begin a life of wealth, health, and peace. You are well-equipped to tap into the knowledge within, release your inner strength, and manifest your purpose. I've met many people like you ready to harness their intuition and excel. This is why I've created a support group to help you do it.

Change can be difficult to navigate, especially at first. However, with the right system in place, anyone can soar. This is why I created the Mach IV Transformation, an online community for members ready to receive the support, guidance, compassion, and love needed to find and express what's true for them. The truth is within us all.

When the right questions are asked, you can start creating life on your terms and begin the journey to achieve your highest purpose. The awesome power of discovering the truth—what's true for you is right for you, and, no one can tell you what it is because it's *your* truth. I, along with other members of the Mach IV Transformation

Community can help you get there so you can experience, grow, and live the greatest vision you have for your life.

Your Faith Heals You

In the Bible you can read about the many works of Jesus Christ and see how his ministry involved the restoration of faith in the ill. One scripture verse found in Matthew 9:22 reads, "But Jesus turned him about and when he saw her, he said, 'Daughter, be of good comfort; thy faith has made thee whole.' And the woman was made whole from that hour."

There are no requirements for healing; it only asks you to believe there are solutions to all problems. Remember, there's no judgment in healing. It's simply a shift from suffering in one space of pain to living and enjoying another space of love, wholeness and joy. When healing is your focus, compassion is the building block for a strong spiritual foundation. No matter what you've struggled with, it will be met at the Mach IV Transformation Community with understanding, acceptance, and love. The community encourages positive resolution and compassion. It's a collaborative effort by me and all the members there. Everyone in the group has a mission to solve problems and be supportive so you get and benefit from the brilliance of the group.

One of the greatest things about the Mach IV Transformation Community is you're with a group who are all working to improve the world and make it a better place. This is a conscious evolution of great importance because when you embrace your truth, you encourage others to do the same. You always have someone encouraging you and supporting your growth.

Healing is a personal journey to wholeness, and when it's a real transformation, you never experience hang-ups, uncertainty or feeling like you're powerless. Total certainty comes when you gain clarity about what's needed to create health, peace, and joy in your life. Confidence arrives when you're no longer "stuck" with physical or spiritual ailments preventing you from living life on your terms because you'll have the answers needed for your personal journey. You never have to wait for someone to "fix" you. This is empowered living; this is living your truth full out so you can enjoy the highest and best of what you want to manifest.

Anything's possible for you. The only thing that can stop you from living your truth, creating your life, and healing now are the beliefs you hold onto. Regardless of what anyone tells you, your beliefs are influencing your life today and change can only occur when you change your belief system. Many people live their lives by chance. Some people live their lives day by day without aim or purpose and then there are those who crave positive change.

You Have the Power to Do Something about It

When you believe you deserve the best, you'll manifest ideal opportunities for your life. If you believe you're not good enough, you'll experience hardships and missed moments of joy and harmony. By changing your belief system, you literally change what comes to you as experiences. You'll attract situations that benefit what you want, and you'll cut the ties of unwanted experiences like lack of money, sickness, fear, etc.

Whatever issue you have, whatever you're struggling with now, you can change instantly by adopting a new perspective. You have the power within to exude greater self-confidence, obtain happiness and reach your destiny, which is greatness. No matter what your circumstances are today, you can stop the negativity, kick physical and spiritual brokenness to the curb and accelerate your life on the fast track to wholeness.

Your truth is unique to you. When you embrace it and live it, you inspire others to do the same, and transformation will naturally occur. The answers are within you. Take a moment to listen, and you'll never have to wait for someone else to rescue you.

Tool Eight: Finding the Answers within You

Grab a pen and paper and quickly write down the first thing that comes to your mind and remember, don't hold anything back. Think of something presently causing you stress or discomfort like money, relationships, or your job and answer these questions. How will

- ...peace feel to you right now?
- ...peace transform your situation now?
- ...calmness feel to you right now?
- ...calmness transform your situation right now?

There's hope and justice if you have been counted as "less than perfect." It's through your struggle that you finally see WHY you're remarkable and worthy of justification. We all cheer on people who have worked hard, are determined, and have cultivated a mindset to succeed. When you win, the emotional high you experience seems sweeter and warranted. Give yourself a big, "Hell yeah!" because you deserve to win, you've earned it through having the heart to win.

In *A Return to Love*, Marianne Williamson wrote:

> ...Our deepest fear is not that we are inadequate.
>
> Our deepest fear is that we are powerful beyond measure.
>
> It is our light, not our darkness, that most frightens us.
>
> We ask ourselves, who am I to be brilliant, gorgeous, talented, and fabulous?
>
> Actually, who are you not to be?
>
> You are a child of God. Your playing small doesn't serve the world.
>
> There's nothing enlightened about shrinking so that other people won't feel insecure around you.
>
> We are all meant to shine, as children do.
>
> We were born to make manifest the glory of God that is within us.
>
> It's not just in some of us; it's in everyone.
>
> As we let our own light shine, we unconsciously give other people permission to do the same.
>
> As we're liberated from our own fear, our presence automatically liberates others...

We often hear stories of people who watched their mother struggle to support the family, or how living in a trailer park didn't represent their true desires. There are many who rose up and challenged "the status quo" because a change was needed in their country or religion. There are many today who want to provide a better life for their children and want a social change to help the struggling.

The point here is each underdog we have valued or held in high esteem found their *personal why* for change. They were motivated by factors that surrounded them and found trust in themselves to strive for success.

With compassion, I strongly identify with the underdog. I was clearly marked for failure at many stages of my life because my body and mind were weak and frail. My mind was plagued by fear and I'm sure if you said, "Boo!" I would have jumped out of my skin. I adopted irrational fears from all my life experiences and the abuse, and then played them in my mind until they permeated every facet of my life and my being. I discounted my body as able to carry a child to term because I experienced so much loss and pain. I was on the brink of suicide for a long time because I felt worthless.

Seriously, I believed there was no hope for someone like me. I already considered this to be factual, but grace overflowed and picked me up.

My turning point arrived in the form of a simple question the first energy healer asked me, "Do you want it?" This simple question created a profound effect on my health and on how I thought about myself and the world around me. I was under the false belief that suffering was my lot in life, my destiny, and illness would always be a factor in my life. My weak physical condition adversely influenced my mental state and I was at the effect of my life rather than the Creator of my life.

However, this one question was the motivation for positive change for me. It was my inspiration to dive deep within, dig past my deepest fear and create peace, happiness, and the skill to overcome any obstacle. Through this process I found *my why* and my purpose. I didn't need others to agree with my choices. I wasn't in search of approval from family and friends in regard to my personal beliefs. I wasn't shameful about my past, and I found the strength to live in compassion every day. Change and motivation arrived for me in the form of a simple question.

My life experience is not the sum total of physical abuse, sexual abuse, or illness. Rather it's a story of triumph and victory over a poor belief system that did not work for me anymore. Once I discovered my beliefs were the real catalyst for change and growth, I developed a healing program and amazing system which is breaking the mold. It's simple, easy-to-use, and it eradicates self-limiting thoughts and illness to create health, wealth, and prosperity. The creation of our existence is built on how we *feel and think* and not solely on our experiences.

Radical change happens when we embrace our personal truth and shun the voices of authority or expertise that don't support our higher purpose. Consider, when you were little—did you believe in a "Boogey Man" and then discovered he wasn't real? Many of us believed in him, but once we learned the truth, he was fictional and disappeared. We let it go and adopted a new belief. It's that simple. The same example applies to life in *anything we pursue;* our personal mindset influences our outcome.

Your Higher Purpose Is in the Expression of You

This is why I'm writing this book to you. We're full of energy. With a simple, practical, technique, the last one in this book, I'll show you how to finally harness your thoughts and design your life with purpose. If you're not careful, your thoughts can transcend the physical realm. When you accept what you see and experience it as the final result for your life, you may not be pleased with the outcome. To live authentically, rise above what you see, hear, and feel. Achieving success means embracing a higher purpose which is your belief system.

The real you, the highest and best you, exists in the freedom to fully express your experiences, beliefs, wants, and desires. Your authentic voice will arrive the moment you decide you'll no longer compromise. Your inner truth will shine outwardly when you share what's real for you with love, compassion, and determination. Healing begins when you acknowledge you're whole and complete, even when the physical realm hasn't caught up to this truth. At any given moment you can change and realign your life with the truth you dare to master.

This is a big step for some, and I was scared to take that leap of faith, too. I lived in fear I'd lose everyone I loved in the afterlife if I didn't include my family's religious tradition in my life. I felt cast down by God and was convinced I would suffer for a long time because He didn't love me.

As you've heard me say in these pages, healing took place when I shifted my perspective and chose to see things differently. I decided it was time to embrace the truth—I'm loved and I can live with compassion towards myself and others. Is it time for you to embrace your truth, too? As you have read and shared my journey, have you been thinking about what your truth is for you?

Truth isn't based on whether you answer to or worship the Universe, Mother Earth, God, or a Spirit. Truth is based on knowing what you say is real. That includes what you see, think, and feel. Your integrity is based on the courage you have to share your truth with others. It's a big shift in thinking, an awakening, and a transformative journey. When the door opened for me, I saw a whole new world that included wholeness, fertility, and peace. I'm not that different from you. In fact, you probably have a wonderful story to share to inspire others to achieve their personal truth and heal from any thought that damages their mind, body, and spirit.

You may have heard the saying, "Life doesn't have a roadmap?"

My feelings about that expression are, "You create your life on purpose."

While I don't have *your* ideal roadmap, I can certainly give you the pen and paper to start charting it out, figuratively speaking. As I mentioned in earlier chapters, my unique system is specifically designed to create a paradigm shift in your life for receiving answers in alignment with *your* truth, healing, increasing your self-confidence, and building trust in yourself.

Can you imagine the impact of embracing new beliefs that serve your higher purpose in life and foster healing and peace of mind?

Time and again I've seen my clients transform and their lives changed. They're now healed and have a renewed faith in their ability to get what they want from life. This isn't to say they've all arrived at their final destination and their lives are all roses and sunshine. This is to say today, when struggles arise, when they meet challenges. When life seems overwhelming, instead of giving up or checking out, they have the tools to overcome and heal resulting in quickly continuing the course they've mapped out for themselves.

I share with my clients how to grab hold of the courage and strength to create positive change. I use an easy approach with simple and direct questions bypassing your "normal" way of thinking and tapping into the *heart* of the matter. I discovered we have the innate power to:

- Heal those pesky, annoying body ailments causing pain and draining your energy
- Remove the mental blocks that cause depression, sadness, anger, and grief
- Tap into your inner truth so you can let your light shine and live with purpose

It's awesome, right? Not only does changing your belief systems create a better existence, especially when your old beliefs don't serve your higher purpose, but you'll no longer need to rely on anyone else to "fix" you.

This isn't to say you travel the road alone now, never asking for help from others. It means you have the tools to take care of many things in your life without searching for someone to help you. On the big stuff you can't seem to overcome on your own, you can have a community of others to help you see your world differently so you can overcome.

I'll share the tools I used to transform my health and my life any time you need do-it-yourself help and support.

Empower Yourself and Live Your Truth

Why is it so important to empower yourself with a healthy mindset? Some of the benefits available in doing so include:

- Reconnecting with your inner self again
- Reestablishing your beliefs—maybe for the first time
- Renewing your mind to gain a new perspective
- Living your truth and trusting you can make your best decisions

With a renewed mind, you'll no longer need a family member or friend to "save you." Instead you can relax, assured in your ability to arrive at decisions that fit you best. When you design your own reality by living what's true for you, you'll tap into your intuition, that small voice within, for guidance and support whenever you need it. Whatever illness you may experience, whatever body part needs healing or emotional upset you have, you'll be the first one on the scene to assess and handle it. You will persist and achieve personal satisfaction much more quickly.

Most importantly, you'll discover the fine art of granting yourself permission to experience you and share your authentic, true self with others without fear, shame or guilt.

Although you'll gain the tools of "fixing you," you won't be alone because when you join the Mach IV Transformation Community, you join forces with like-minded people supporting your journey. They will help you as you need assistance, and as you help them you will grow stronger and more capable.

Mach IV Transformation is a conscious community of individuals who want and desire encouragement through the discovery process, some of the questions I've shared throughout this book, and much more. We're a group of people who show compassion no matter what you've done in your past or what kind of trials you're experiencing now. We're simply here to help build a foundation for accelerated growth of your well-being mentally, physically, and spiritually. We support your right to become more than you are today with no shame or guilt about any past transgressions or weaknesses. The Mach IV Transformation Community embraces all you are right now and what you choose to become tomorrow and going forward. When you join, you can expect:

- A transformed life: Build and watch your wealth increase, peace abound, and know you can create good things to happen.
- Healing and good vibes: Discover the hidden thoughts triggering illness and find relief from negativity once and for all.
- A shift from powerless to powerful: Gain the knowledge and tools to help you manifest the life you want without fear or hesitation.
- Constructive reflection: With poignant questions, you'll tap into ideas and thoughts ready to be discovered and utilized, helping you excel at whatever you choose.

Some people have been waiting twenty years to heal their body, mend their broken heart, or finally step out from the shadows into their own magnificence. Unfortunately, some have gone to their grave waiting for someone else to rescue them from pain, frustration, and agony.

The truth is, only you can turn your life around and decide how it will begin and end from this moment forward. The wonderful part about it is you don't have to navigate through your journey to embrace your truth and your transformation alone. I will take you by the hand and share with you how to transform your life instantly by using Mach IV Transformation. Whatever your need is—healing pain and fatigue, recovery from a loss or grief—I'll provide the tools to empower your life for a quick, virtually painless, positive change for the better.

Join me today and everyone in the Mach IV Transformation Community today for a fast track to healing and mindset transformation.

You'll not only receive the Four Modules I've created to help you master your mind, body, and spirit simultaneously, you'll also receive a mini-class I've created to help you:

- Become self-aware and know what you feel and think
- Kick fear to the curb for good
- Easily forgive yourself and others, no matter what
- Restore broken relationships
- Increase your health and vitality
- ... and much, much more

Join the Mach IV Transformation Community now and gain full access to the group through Facebook. I and all the Mach IV Transformation members would love to help you on your journey and will undoubtedly benefit from your personal experience and wisdom.

http://www.joannaashley.com/mach-iv-transformation/

Please contact me for more information at:
joanna@joannaashley.com

www.ingramcontent.com/pod-product-compliance
Lightning Source LLC
LaVergne TN
LVHW051838080426
835512LV00018B/2947